FASTING

for Breakthrough
& Deliverance

JOHN ECKHARDT

CHARISMA HOUSE

D0905968

Most CHARISMA HOUSE BOOK GROUP products are available at special quantity discounts for bulk purchase for sales promotions, premiums, fund-raising, and educational needs. For details, write Charisma House Book Group, 600 Rinehart Road, Lake Mary, Florida 32746, or telephone (407) 333-0600.

FASTING FOR BREAKTHROUGH AND DELIVERANCE
    by John Eckhardt
Published by Charisma House
Charisma Media/Charisma House Book Group
600 Rinehart Road
Lake Mary, Florida 32746
www.charismahouse.com

Unless otherwise noted, all Scripture quotations are taken from the Holy Bible, Modern English Version. Copyright © 2014 by Military Bible Association. Used by permission. All rights reserved.

Scripture quotations marked AMP are from the Amplified Bible. Copyright © 1954, 1958, 1962, 1964, 1965, 1987 by The Lockman Foundation. Used by permission.

Scripture quotations marked CEV are from the Contemporary English Version, copyright © 1995 by the American Bible Society. Used by permission.

Scripture quotations marked JB are from the Jerusalem Bible, copyright © 1966, Doubleday. Used by permission.

Scripture quotations marked KJV are from the King James Version of the Bible.

Cover design by Justin Evans

Visit the author's website at
http://www.johneckhardtministries.com

Library of Congress Cataloging-in-Publication Data:
An application to register this book for cataloging has been
submitted to the Library of Congress.
International Standard Book Number: 978-1-62998-646-3
E-book ISBN: 978-1-62136-701-9

16 17 18 19 20 — 9876543
Printed in the United States of America

CONTENTS

Chapter 1

EXCEPT BY PRAYER AND FASTING

This kind does not go out except by prayer and fasting.

—MATTHEW 17:21

Y OU'VE COMMANDED, REBUKED, prayed prayers, done warfare, and shouted, but there's more that needs to be broken off your life. It's time to add some fasting to your warfare strategy. There is no other way around some demonic strongholds. No shortcuts. You have to fast and humble yourself until that thing breaks and leaves your life.

Demons are different in terms of their wickedness. There are demons that are stronger, more wicked, unclean, and stubborn, and higher in rank, ability, and intelligence. The longer a demon has been in your family or in your life, the harder it is to remove because its roots go very deep. Demons such as rebellion, pride, witchcraft, Jezebel, poverty, and lack may only come out with a high level of faith.

Sometimes it seems as if they cannot be dislodged, and people will get discouraged and frustrated and feel they have failed. In Matthew 17 the disciples of Jesus encountered a demon in a young boy and could not cure him because of their unbelief. Unbelief hinders us from dealing with strongholds. It takes faith to dislodge the enemy. Fasting helps you overcome unbelief and build strong faith.

This is the supernatural combination that Jesus gave His disciples in Matthew 17: prayer and fasting. I am not saying that when you fast you will earn brownie points with God or that you are working your way to enjoying God's blessings. We don't fast to be saved, please God, or go to heaven. There is no law that says if you don't fast you will go to hell. We fast for breakthrough and revival, for family and loved ones. For the weapons of our warfare are not carnal but mighty through God!

Some things take fasting and prayer. There is no other way around. There are those kinds of demons that just don't give up. They are strong, proud, arrogant, and defiant. They are familiar spirits that have been in your family. But you have to get to the point that you don't care how messed up your family is; you say, "It is stopping with me. This is not going on to another generation. This is it, devil. If my grandmother or grandfather didn't stand against it, if my mother and father didn't defeat it, I'm going to defeat it. I refuse to be poor, broke, sick, rejected, messed up.... No!"

Sometimes you have to do something unusual, extraordinary, and beyond the norm to see breakthrough. Normal church, normal Christianity, normal preaching, and normal praying are not going to get the job done. Some little sweet prayer is not going to do. Religion won't get it done. It is going to take an anointing that destroys the yoke. When you fast, the anointing increases in your life because you are so into the Spirit. The authority of God, power of God, and faith of God comes alive when you lay aside some things and fast. You will find yourself getting stronger and stronger. Shouting doesn't do it. It is the anointing that does it.

Isaiah 58 talks about how we can fast to break every yoke to undo the heavy burdens. Fasting makes room so that the oppressed go free. Fasting breaks bondages and causes revival. When you are dealing with a serious issue—maybe you are dealing with something you don't know how to handle—the best thing to do sometimes is to let go of some food for a little while. Pray against that thing. Man may not be able to help you, and you may not know how to defeat it, but with God all things are possible.

As you fast and humble yourself, the grace of God will come upon your life. The Lord will be the strength of your life. What you could not do in the flesh, you can do by the Spirit of God. Because it's not by might nor by power, but by the Spirit of the Lord that every mountain is removed!

Listen, extraordinary situations require extraordinary measures. Sometimes it only happens when you get desperate— when you are so tired of being defeated and hindered in an area.

Let's see some victories we haven't seen before. Let's get some breakthroughs we haven't had before. Let's see some miracles we haven't seen before. Let's drive out some demons we haven't driven out before. Let's see some curses broken that would not leave. Let's see some generational stuff uprooted that could not be uprooted. Let's see a change! Not once. Not twice. Not even three times. If you have to fast more times than that, do it. Don't give up. Keep doing it. Keep going until you know you have victory, until you have breakthrough, until you sense something breaking!

You have to get so tired of the devil that you say, "Enough is enough. If I have to turn my plate down to get a breakthrough in this area, I won't eat." When your stomach starts screaming out, tell it to back up. In the end, you will win and have victory! Let our spiritual enemies be smitten and consumed in Jesus's name!

You have to be determined: "No demon is going to control my life. I am a child of God, and who the Son sets free is free indeed. I don't care how stubborn this thing is, how it tries to hang on. I am going to break every finger and thumb of the enemy. I'm going to break his wrists, break his grip. . . . Devil, you cannot have my life!" This is the faith and unshakable resolve fasting will build in your life to see deliverance in every area the enemy has tried to control.

HOW TO FAST

Fasting is beneficial whether you fast partially or fully. One-day fasts on a consistent basis will strengthen your spirit over time and give you the ability to disciple yourself for longer fasts. Three-day fasts with just water are a powerful way to see breakthroughs. Esther and the people of Israel went into a three-day fast when they were seeking deliverance from death at the hand of Haman, the king's evil advisor (Esther 4:16). Fasts longer than three days should be done by people with more experience in fasting.

I do not recommend long fasts unless there is an emergency or if one is led by the Holy Spirit to do so. Daniel fasted twenty-one days and saw a great breakthrough for his people (Dan. 9–10). Daniel was also a prophet, and God will use prophets to fast for different reasons to see breakthroughs. Jesus fasted forty days before beginning His ministry (Matt. 4:1–2). Moses and Elijah also fasted forty days (Exod. 34:28; Deut. 9:9, 18; 1 Kings 19:8). I do know of people who have fasted forty days and have seen great breakthroughs.

A partial fast can include some food such as vegetables and can be done for long lengths. Complete fasts consist of only water, and water is important to cleanse the system of toxins that are released through fasting. The Holy Spirit will reveal to you when you need to fast. A fasted lifestyle is a powerful lifestyle.

APPROACH FASTING WITH HUMILITY AND SINCERITY

In Jesus's day the Pharisees fasted with attitudes of pride and superiority:

> The Pharisee stood and prayed thus with himself, God, I thank thee, that I am not as other men are....I fast twice in the week...
>
> —LUKE 18:11–12, KJV

Anytime you are full of pride, being legalistic and religious, you can fast and pray all you want, but you won't see many miracles. The Pharisees didn't have any miracles come as a result of their prayer and fasting. They had no power. Jesus had all the miracles because He was humble and full of mercy, love, and compassion toward people.

The Pharisees had nothing but long robes on—robes with no miracles. They couldn't heal a headache, a mosquito bite, or a hangnail. They had no power because they were not humble and showed no mercy. Jesus showed up and broke all their rules. He healed the sick, raised the dead, and cast out devils. Then they wanted to kill him. They were not concerned about people. They were more concerned about their position and their title. Don't ever get to a place where your position or title takes the humility and the mercy of God out of your life. Always be humble. Always be merciful.

We must approach fasting with humility. Fasting must be genuine and not religious or hypocritical. This is what God requires in fasting. We must have correct motives in fasting. Fasting is a powerful tool if done correctly. Muslims and Hindus fast, but their fasts are merely religious. Great miracles and breakthroughs happen when fasting is done in the right spirit.

Isaiah chapter 58 describes the fast that God has chosen:

+ Fasting cannot be done with amusement (v. 3).
+ Fasting cannot be done while mistreating others (v. 3).
+ Fasting cannot be done for strife or contention (v. 4).
+ Fasting should cause one to bow his head in humility, like a bulrush (v. 5).
+ Fasting should be a time of searching the heart and repenting (v. 5).
+ Fasting should be done with an attitude of compassion for the lost and hurting (v. 7).

This is the fast that God promises to bless.

The enemy knows the power of prayer and fasting, and he will do everything in his power to stop you. Believers who begin to fast can expect to encounter much spiritual resistance. A believer must be committed to a fasted lifestyle. The rewards of fasting far outweigh the obstacles of the enemy.

FASTING BRINGS AN OPEN REWARD

Fasting has great rewards. Many believers are unaware of the great rewards that come through fasting. Understanding the great benefits of fasting will motivate more believers to make it a regular part of their lives. Matthew 6:17–18 says, "But you, when you fast, anoint your head and wash your face, so that you will not appear to men to be fasting, but to your Father who is in secret. And your Father who sees in secret will reward you openly."

God promises rewards to those who fast in secret. Reward is God's favor, abundance, and blessing. The open rewards of fasting include blessing, abundance, favor, and prosperity. Learn the secret of obtaining God's reward through private fasting. Everybody doesn't need to know you are fasting. As you are led by the Holy Spirit, make this a personal discipline between you and God and see how He rewards you.

> And without faith it is impossible to please God, for he who comes to God must believe that He exists and that He is a rewarder of those who diligently seek Him.
> —HEBREWS 11:6

DECLARE THE BENEFITS OF FASTING OVER YOUR LIFE

Lord, I believe in the power of Your chosen fast (Isa. 58).

Lord, let my fasting destroy the yokes that the enemy has set up against me.

Let Your light come into my life through Your chosen fast.

Let health and healing be released to me through Your chosen fast.

Let me see breakthroughs of salvation and deliverance in my life through Your chosen fast.

Let miracles be released in my life through Your chosen fast.

Let Your power and authority be released in my life through Your chosen fast.

I humble my soul through fasting; let Your favor exalt me.

I drive every stubborn demon out of my life through Your chosen fast.

Let Your covenant blessing and mercy be released on me through Your chosen fast.

Nothing is impossible with You, Lord; let my impossibilities become possibilities through Your chosen fast.

Let every assignment of hell against me be broken through Your chosen fast.

Let all pride, rebellion, and witchcraft operating in my life be destroyed through Your chosen fast.

Let Your anointing increase in my life through Your chosen fast.

Let me enjoy restoration through Your chosen fast.

Let all carnality be rebuked from my life through Your chosen fast.

Let all habits and iniquity in me be broken and overcome through Your chosen fast.

Let my prayers be answered speedily through Your chosen fast.

Guide me through Your chosen fast.

Manifest Your glory to me through Your chosen fast.

Let the strongholds of sexual impurity and lust be broken in my life through Your chosen fast.

Let sickness and infirmity be destroyed in my life, and let healing come forth through Your chosen fast.

Let all poverty and lack be destroyed in my life through Your chosen fast.

Remove all oppression and torment from my life through Your chosen fast.

I humble myself with fasting (Ps. 35:13).

I will turn to the Lord with fasting, weeping, and mourning (Joel 2:12).

This "kind" that I face will go out from me through fasting and prayer (Matt. 17:21).

I will fast according to the fast chosen by the Lord (Isa. 58:5).

I will proclaim a fast and humble myself before our God, to seek from Him the right way for my family and all our possessions (Ezra 8:21).

I fast to loose the bonds of wickedness, to undo heavy burdens, to let the oppressed go free, and to break every yoke (Isa. 58:6).

I will set my face toward the Lord God to make requests by prayer and supplication, with fasting, sackcloth, and ashes (Dan. 9:3).

I will fast in the secret place, and my Father sees in secret. He will reward me openly (Matt. 6:18).

I will not depart from the temple of the Lord but will serve God with fastings and prayers night and day (Luke 2:37).

Chapter 2

BREAK EVERY CHAIN

The breaker is come up before them: they have broken up, and
have passed through the gate, and are gone out by it: and their king
shall pass before them, and the LORD on the head of them.

—MICAH 2:13, KJV

T HERE ARE SOME things in our lives that just can't stay around if we are to walk victoriously and in covenant with God. We have gone too long and too soft with the enemy wreaking havoc in our lives. Fasting can release the breaker anointing. The prophet Micah prophesied the day of the breaker coming up before his people. We are living in the days of the breaker.

The Lord is a breaker. He is able to break through any obstacle or opposition on behalf of His covenant people. There is a breaker anointing arising upon the church. We are seeing and experiencing more breakthroughs than ever before. Fasting will cause breakthroughs to continue in families, cities, nations, finances, church growth, salvation, healing, and deliverance. It will help believers to break through all opposition from the enemy.

As I have said, there are some spirits operating in our lives that cannot be overcome without fasting. Some believers struggle with certain limitations that they cannot seem to break through. A revelation of fasting will change this and result in victories that would not ordinarily be obtained. A life of consistent fasting will cause many victories to manifest. God's will is that every believer lives a life of victory with nothing being impossible to them.

There are stubborn spirits that will only respond to fasting and prayer. We will talk about the nature of such spirits in the next chapter. And throughout the book in chapters 5–30 I will focus on areas of demonic oppression or distress that can reach such a level in a person's life that they are not easily broken except through fasting and prayer. We all may deal with problems in life from time to time and they may quickly pass over or get resolved, but the issues I am bringing out in this book are long-lasting, deeply entrenched issues for which you have been seeking breakthrough and have yet to find peace, victory, or hear a word from the Lord on it. I am talking about things like generational strongholds that tenaciously hold on to families and nations for years or waiting and waiting to hear from God on a certain issue or decision and heaven seems silent. Fasting will break these strongholds that stand in your way to receiving from the Lord. These strongholds include poverty, sickness, witchcraft, sexual impurity, pride, fear, confusion, and marital problems. Fasting will help you to overcome these strongholds and break free from your limitations.

As a believer deliverance and freedom are part of your salvation package. The enemy fights you for this freedom. This is why we are in a battle. He continues to steal from you what has already been claimed for you. Jesus gave you the authority to stop him from taking what God has already said is yours.

ACCOMPANY YOUR FASTING WITH POWERFUL PRAYER

There's little point to spiritual fasting without focused and intense prayer directed toward an issue or situation. Prayer is a powerful weapon for believers who have a hatred for the works of darkness (Ps. 139:21). Do you hate every false way (Ps. 119:104)? When you have the fear of the Lord you will hate evil (Prov. 8:13), and your righteous prayers will reflect it.

Because you hate evil and love what is good, your warfare prayers will not only be for victory in your city, region, or nation, but they will also be targeted toward seeing breakthrough in your personal life. Your prayers can demolish strongholds.

When you pray, you are enforcing the victory over Satan that was won at the Cross. You are executing the judgments written against him through your prayers. You are reinforcing the fact that principalities and powers have been spoiled (Col. 2:15). This honor is given to all His saints.

This is why it is so unfortunate that there are so many believers who struggle with prayer. Many say they don't know how to pray. Some have become discouraged in prayer. This is why there are still so many areas in their lives that are still under oppression of the enemy. The Lord taught me a long time ago the importance of praying the Word to overcome spiritual resistance to the plan of God for my life. The Holy Spirit has helped me understand many scriptures and how to use them in prayer so that I can continue to walk in victory. You will see these prayers throughout this book specifically placed in each area to help spark your own prayers in the area in which you need breakthrough.

When you base your prayers on the Word of God, it will inspire you to pray. Praying the Word of God will expand your ability to pray. It will stir up a spirit of prayer within you. We are told to pray with all kinds of prayers (Eph. 6:18). Praying the Word will cause you to pray many different kinds of prayers that you ordinarily would not have prayed. This will help to break the limitations off your prayer life. Reading, studying, and meditating on the promises of God will motivate you to pray. God has given many great and precious promises—promises to help you, to save and deliver you from the hand of the enemy, and to heal you and prosper you. It is through faith-filled prayer that you inherit these covenant promises (Heb. 6:12).

Prayer is also one of the ways we release the will of God upon the earth. We must study the Word of God in order to know the will of God. This is why prayer and the Word must be combined. Daniel was able to pray effectively because he knew the word of God concerning His people (Dan. 9:2–3).

We should pray with understanding (1 Cor. 14:15). Understanding the will of God will help us pray correctly. The Word of God is the will of God. We are not to be unwise; we are to understand what the will of the Lord is (Eph. 5:17). Prayer also helps us walk perfectly and completely in all the will of God (Col. 4:12).

We are encouraged to call upon the Lord. He has promised to show us great and mighty things (Jer. 33:3). The Lord delights in our prayers. He delights in answering our prayers. Before we call, He will answer (Isa. 65:24). The Lord's ears are open unto the prayers of the righteous (1 Pet. 3:12). The effectual fervent prayer of a righteous man avails much (James 5:16). We are told to pray without ceasing (1 Thess. 5:17).

Our God hears prayer. All flesh should come to Him in prayer (Ps. 65:2). All believers have similar challenges, and all believers can overcome these challenges through prayer. God is no respecter of persons (Acts 10:34). He is near to all who call upon Him (Ps. 145:19). The Lord will hear your supplication and will receive your prayers (Ps. 6:9). Calling upon the

Lord will bring salvation and deliverance from your enemies (Ps. 18:3). This has always been a key to deliverance. You can pray yourself out of any adverse situation. The Lord is your helper. God will not turn away your prayers (Ps. 66:20). God will not despise your prayers (Ps. 102:17). The prayers of the upright are God's delight (Prov. 15:8).

God has promised to make us joyful in the house of prayer (Isa. 56:7). God's house is called a house of prayer for all nations. I believe we should not only pray but also enjoy prayer. The joy of the Lord is our strength. Prayer should yield an abundance of miracles and rewards. Those who enjoy the results of prayer will enjoy an exciting life.

David was a king who understood the place of prayer in victory. He had many victories over his enemies. He saw mighty deliverance through prayer. He prayed for the defeat of his enemies and God answered him. We will have the same results over our spiritual enemies. We are not wrestling against flesh and blood. We must overcome principalities and powers with the armor of God. We must take the sword of the Spirit and pray with all prayer (Eph. 6:12–18).

The prayers of David ended with Psalm 72:20. He ended them by praying that the whole earth would be filled with God's glory. This is the end of prayer. We believe that the earth will be filled with the knowledge of the glory of the Lord as the waters cover the sea (Hab. 2:14). This is our goal. We will continue to pray toward the fulfillment of this promise. We will see the growth of God's kingdom and the destruction of the powers of darkness through our prayers. Revival and glory are increasing. Our prayers are like gasoline to the fire.

Our faith-filled prayers coupled with times of periodic

fasting are keys to seeing miracles and breakthrough on a consistent basis. Whatever we ask in prayer, believing, we will receive (Matt. 21:22).

PRAYERS THAT BREAK THE POWERS OF DARKNESS

Let the Assyrian be broken in my land (Isa. 14:25).

Break in pieces the gates of brass, and cut the bars of iron (Isa. 45:2).

I break every yoke from off my neck, and I burst all the bonds in the name of Jesus (Jer. 30:8).

Break them with the rod of iron, and dash them in pieces like a potter's vessel (Ps. 2:9).

Break the arm of the wicked (Ps. 10:15).

Break their teeth, O God, in their mouths. Break the teeth of the young lions (Ps. 58:6).

Let the oppressor be broken in pieces (Ps. 72:4).

Let the arms of the wicked be broken (Ps. 37:17).

Let the horns of the wicked be broken (Dan. 8:8).

Let the kingdoms of darkness be broken (Dan. 11:4).

Let the foundations of the wicked be broken (Ezek. 30:4).

Let the kingdoms of Babylon be broken (Jer. 51:58).

Let all the bows of the wicked be broken (Ps. 37:14).

I break in pieces the horse and the rider (Jer. 51:21).

I break in pieces the chariot and the rider (Jer. 51:21).

I break in pieces the captains and the rulers (Jer. 51:23).

Let Your Word out of my mouth be like a hammer that breaks the rocks in pieces (Jer. 23:29).

Break down every wall erected by the enemy against my life (Ezek. 13:14).

I break down every altar erected by the enemy against my life in the name of Jesus (Hos. 10:2).

Let the idols and images of the land be broken by Your power, O Lord (Deut. 7:5).

I break and disannul every demonic covenant made by my ancestors in the name of Jesus (Isa. 28:18).

Chapter 3

FASTING DESTROYS STUBBORN DEMONS AND STRONGHOLDS

If you have faith as a grain of mustard seed, you will say to this mountain, "Move from here to there," and it will move. And nothing will be impossible for you. But this kind does not go out except by prayer and fasting.

—MATTHEW 17:20–21

GOD WANTS TO break and destroy some stubborn stuff in your life. Deliverance from all your enemies is a benefit of walking in covenant with God. He wants to set you free from all the wiles of the devil, even the ones you think you will never be free of. I'm talking about stubborn problems that don't seem to move or break no matter how much you pray and war, stuff that just doesn't seem to let go. A lot of people have become frustrated and discouraged because it just wears them out. But God has a plan for your deliverance, a way of escape out of the snares and traps of the enemy. The Lord says:

> *"In an acceptable time I have heard you, and in the day of salvation* I have helped you." Look, now is the accepted time; look, *now is the day of salvation.*
>
> —2 CORINTHIANS 6:2, EMPHASIS ADDED

> Do not be afraid. Stand firm and you will see the deliverance the LORD will bring you today.
>
> —EXODUS 14:13, NIV

"THIS KIND"

As I mentioned briefly in chapter 2, there are different kinds of demons. Some demons are very easy to cast out of your life. Some demons always put up a fight. It takes a lot more strength and anointing to break their power. In Matthew 17 there is the story of the man who brought his child to the disciples of Jesus and they could not cure him.

> Jesus rebuked the demon, and he came out of him. And the child was healed instantly. Then the disciples came to Jesus privately and said, "Why could we not cast him out?" Jesus said to them, "Because of your unbelief. For truly I say to you, if you have faith as a grain of mustard seed, you will say to this mountain, 'Move from here to there,' and it will move. And nothing will be impossible for you. However, this kind does not go out except by prayer and fasting."
>
> —MATTHEW 17:18–21

The scripture says "this kind," which helps us know that there are different kinds of demons. Some demons are stronger than others. Some demons are more stubborn and defiant than others. There are a lot of reasons why a spirit can be stubborn in a person's life.

Sometimes these things can be so deeply rooted, strong, and stubborn, because not only have they been in your life but they have also been in your family's life for generations. Sometimes a demon in a person's life is like a plant that has a complex root system. The deeper the roots go in the soil, the harder it is to pull up the plant. And sometimes people have had spirits in their lives for so many years until they have developed strong root systems. When they try to pull them out, they don't come out by just tugging at them. They need to get in the root system and cut it and then pull them out.

If you have a green thumb or have done any gardening, then you know all weeds are not the same. You can come across a weed and pull and pull and that thing won't budge. It's been there so long its roots go deep into the soil. When I say "stubborn," I am not referring to stubbornness, which is a demon in itself. I am referring to a spirit that is very difficult to remove. Jesus gives us the key, which is prayer and fasting. If you are having any of these issues in your life, I believe that prayer and fasting are the way to break their power and drive them out of your life. There is just no way around it.

FACING GOLIATH

When we face stubborn demons and strongholds, it's as if we are facing Goliaths. All of Israel was intimidated by Goliath because he was a giant. He challenged anybody to come down and fight him for forty days and forty nights. Nobody met the challenge until David showed up. David said, "Who is this uncircumcised Philistine who would dare to defy the armies of the living God? I'll go and fight him!" (See 1 Samuel 17:26.) David was a fighter. And I pray the spirit of David would come upon you in this hour. Every time a Goliath stands up and challenges you, I pray that you will say, "God has not given me the spirit of fear but of power and love and a sound mind." And as David did, may you not only kill the enemy but also cut off his head!

Think about David's weapons. He tried to use King Saul's armor, but it was too big and heavy. He went to battle with his own little slingshot. A slingshot? Against a giant? Sometimes the weapons God gives us to fight with and defeat the enemy are most unusual. But "the weapons of our warfare are not carnal, but mighty through God to the pulling down of strongholds" (2 Cor. 10:4). Use the weapon of praise. Use the weapon of worship. Use the weapon of the Word. Use the weapon of prayer and fasting. Declare: "I am not trying to do this in my flesh. God, I pray. I fast. I humble myself before You. I know that it's not by might nor by power but by the Spirit of the Lord that every mountain be removed from my life!"

It is time to be free from every stubborn devil and stubborn person who tries to keep you from doing what God has called you to do. Stand up and say, "No, devil, 'this kind' will leave. I will pray and fast until I get a breakthrough. Because I will not allow anything to stop me from doing what God has assigned for me to do."

DON'T LOSE HOPE

One of my favorite scriptures is, "Hope deferred makes the heart sick, but when the desire comes, it is a tree of life" (Prov. 13:12). In other words, when you have hope for something to come to pass but it keeps getting deferred, you get discouraged and feel like giving up. But when the desire comes and you get what you had been hoping and believing for, you feel alive and invigorated—fulfilled. The Bible calls this "a tree of life."

One of the keys to enjoying life, the abundant life, and enjoying the life in God is to have your hopes come to pass. When you are always left in a place of hoping and hoping, this deferral turns into hopelessness, discouragement, frustration, depression, and torment. When people can't seem to get breakthrough in particular areas, they just give up. Some have left church or left God because this thing they were hoping would break through was so stubborn and would not move in their lives. But I am committed to seeing stubborn demons and strongholds destroyed. No matter how strong or stubborn a demon is, God still has all power!

One of the most defiant and stubborn animals is the mule. If mules don't want to do something, you can't make them do it. They just dig in. You have to drag them. My prayer is that through this book, and others to follow, I am giving you tools and strategies from God to deal with mule spirits, donkey demons, and all those demons that say no when you say come out (sometimes they say no before you say come out). They will come out in the name of Jesus and through prayer and fasting.

PRAYERS TO BREAK STUBBORN DEMONS AND STRONGHOLDS

I bind, rebuke, and cast out every stubborn demon that would attempt to stubbornly hold on to my life in the name of Jesus.

I come against every stubborn stronghold and command it to yield to the power of God and the name of Jesus (2 Sam. 5:7).

I put pressure on every stubborn demon and stronghold and break its grip in my life in the name of Jesus.

I uproot every stubborn root from my life in the name of Jesus (Matt. 15:13).

I command every stubborn, iron-like yoke to shatter and break in the name of Jesus (Judg. 1:19).

I break the power of every proud, stubborn, and arrogant demon that exalts itself against Christ, and command it to be abased, in the name of Jesus.

I break the power of all iniquity in my family that would stubbornly attempt to control my life in the name of Jesus.

I come against all obstinate demons and break their influence in my life in the name of Jesus.

I rebuke all stubborn, habitual patterns of failure and frustration in my life in the name of Jesus.

I rebuke all stubborn pharaohs that would attempt to hold God's people, and I command you to let God's people go, in the name of Jesus (Exod. 8:32).

I bind and rebuke all stubborn enemies, who stubbornly oppose me and my progress, in the name of Jesus.

I rebuke all stubborn demons that would attempt to resist the power of God and the authority I have through Jesus Christ, and I render you powerless to resist, in the name of Jesus.

I come against every persistent pattern that limits me, and I render it powerless against me, in the name of Jesus.

There is nothing impossible through faith, and I release my faith against every stubborn and obstinate demon, and I resist you steadfastly, in the name of Jesus (Matt. 19:26).

I weaken, break down, and pressure every stubborn demon and stronghold. You are getting weaker and weaker, and I am getting stronger and stronger. I exercise long war against you, until you are completely defeated and destroyed from my life in the name of Jesus (2 Sam. 3:1).

I lay siege against every stubborn stronghold through prayer and fasting, until your walls come down in the name of Jesus (Deut. 20:19).

I use the battering ram of prayer and fasting to demolish all the gates of every stubborn stronghold in the name of Jesus. Let every Jericho wall fall through my praise, as I lift my voice as a trumpet against you in the name of Jesus (Josh. 6:1, 20).

Let every demonic stump be removed from my life in the name of Jesus.

I break the will of every stubborn spirit that would attempt to remain in my life in the name of Jesus. You have no will to remain, your will is broken, and you must submit to the name of Jesus and the power of the Holy Ghost.

I come against all stubborn demons and strongholds in my family that have refused to leave, and I assault every demonic fortress that has been built for generations, in the name of Jesus.

I rebuke every stubborn mule and bull of Bashan from my life in the name of Jesus. I break your will against me in the name of Jesus. You are defeated and must bow to the name above all names (Ps. 22:12).

The anointing is increasing in my life through prayer and fasting, and every stubborn yoke is being destroyed (Isa. 10:27).

Chapter 4

FASTING INCREASES YOUR STRENGTH IN LONG WAR

Now there was a long war between the house of Saul and the house of David. But David grew stronger and stronger, and the house of Saul grew weaker and weaker.

—2 SAMUEL 3:1, NKJV

YOU MAY NOT like this term *long war*. I don't blame you. Who would? We want it to end quickly. But some wars don't end quickly. If you are fighting a stubborn enemy who refuses to give in to surrender, then just know it is going to fight and fight and fight. There are demons who fight and fight and fight to hold on. But I have good news for you. If you keep putting pressure on the enemy, you will get stronger and stronger, and he will get weaker and weaker.

What demons cannot handle is a long war. They want you to hit them and give up. But you have the mentality that you will continue in prayer, fasting, and putting pressure on this demon, because it is just a matter of time before it breaks!

Sometimes you have to weaken demons. We have experienced this in our deliverance ministry at Crusaders Church. We've dealt with demons that are very strong. Over a period of time we will pray, fast, rebuke, and hold several sessions dealing with the same demon, but after a while we'll see that demon getting weaker and weaker.

When you first start praying for deliverance from some demonic spirits, they will tell you, "We aren't going. You can't cancel/cast us out. You don't have power. We're going to stay here. We are going to destroy. You belong to us. This is our house." You just say, "OK. Just keep talking. I'm going to pray—pray in tongues, fast, rebuke the devil, plead the blood, quote scriptures..." Then after a while those same tough-talking demons will say, "Would you leave us alone? Would you give it a break? You are getting on our nerves." You can always tell when demons are starting to weaken, because they get angry and start threatening. They'll say, "We're going to kill you." Don't be afraid. That's called panic. When you start seeing the devil panic, you know that you need to keep putting on the pressure until he whimpers out of your life.

Just because it's a long war does not mean you are losing. People have asked me why God would allow certain things to stay in our lives for long periods of time. God allows it because He wants to teach us how to fight. You learn faith and persistence in long war. You need that as a child of God. You need to learn how to stand in faith against impossible situations. You don't look at how it looks. You need to believe God.

When God sent Israel into the land to drive out the enemy, they did not drive all of them out in one year. God didn't let them drive all of the enemies out of the land in one year. Verse two in Judges 3 says that God left some of the nations in Canaan to teach Israel how to fight, how to war. Many of the ones that came out of Egypt knew nothing about warfare.

Sometimes as you are battling darkness, the Lord is teaching you how to war, how to use your faith, how to use the Word, how to use prayer, and how to stand. He wants to teach you how to fight so you will not be a wimp in the army of the Lord. The greatest warriors in God's kingdom are people who have had to fight battles for themselves and overcome some things. When you overcome stuff, it is no longer a theory from the Bible. You know that victory is real. You know how to achieve victory. That gives you much better ability to fight for other people, to war for other people, to use your faith, and to develop your strength in the Lord. Sometimes your personal victories set you up to be able to help someone else get victory.

A lot of believers don't like a long war. They give up. This is what the enemy is counting on. He is hoping the people of God will get tired and quit. What he wants us to feel is that we can't do it, that we can't defeat him, and that we won't win. He wants to bluff us that we are not strong enough. But I say to you, don't give up. Don't roll over and die. If God be for you, who can be against you (Rom. 8:31)? God is on your side. You may have to fight for what's yours, and it may take some time. But when you pray and fast and commit to seeing victory no matter how long it takes, it is only a matter of time until the enemy will break, and you will have victory.

No, Three Times Is Not the Charm

In 2 Kings 13:14–19 we are introduced to the arrow of deliverance and learn how the prophetic anointing helps us to war.

> Now Elisha had become sick with the illness of which he would die. So Joash the king of Israel went down to him and wept before him, and said, "My father, my father, the chariot of Israel and its horsemen." Elisha said to him, "Take a bow and arrows." Then he said to the king of Israel, "Draw the bow." So he drew it. Elisha put his hands on the king's hands. Then he said, "Open the east window." So he opened it. Then Elisha said, "Shoot." So he shot. Then he said, "The arrow of the deliverance of the LORD, and the

arrow of deliverance from Aram; for *you must strike Aram in Aphek until you have destroyed them.*" Then he said, "Take the arrows." So he took them. Then he said to the king of Israel, "Strike the ground." So he struck it three times and stood there. Then the man of God was angry with him and said, "You should have struck it five or six times. Then you would have stricken Aram until you had finished them. Now you will strike Aram just three times."

—EMPHASIS ADDED

I believe we can war according to prophecy. The word of the Lord is what you need to win and achieve victory. It is important to be connected to the prophetic. The words encourage us in what we are dealing with. It helps us to war against our enemies and win. The Syrians were the major enemies of Israel. They were a very strong and stubborn enemy. King Joash went to a sick and dying prophet Elisha and cried out to him about the armies of Syria. Elisha told Joash that he must strike against Syria over and over again until they have been destroyed. Then Elisha told him to take a bow and arrows and strike it on the ground. He didn't tell him how many times. Joash hit it on the ground three times and stopped. The prophet was angry because it meant Joash would only defeat the Syrians three times.

Three times was not enough to destroy the Syrians as Elisha had prophesied. Perhaps Elisha could have told him how many times to strike the arrows on the ground. But sometimes what is in a person comes out in their actions. Joash didn't have enough hatred and anger for the enemy to strike the ground beyond the third time—or until the arrow broke!

When you are dealing with the enemy, you need to give him more than just a courtesy tap. You need to really want to win.

You have to hate what you are fighting so much that you beat it until the arrows break. You have to hate lust, poverty, fear, rejection, or whatever it is until you smash it. It's not just one, two, three, and then look at the prophet and ask, "Did I do good?" No! Strike it until it is destroyed!

Another principle: sometimes it takes more than one victory before you completely consume the enemy. It wasn't just one battle; it was more than one. In essence the prophet said, "You should have struck four or five times to completely consume the enemy. Now you will only win three times." And evidently three victories would not be enough to completely destroy the Syrians. The Syrians lost, but they were still in a position to rebuild. We want to destroy the enemy so that he can't rebuild anymore. We want to mess up his strongholds so much that they are destroyed, and we don't have to worry about seeing that thing again.

STUBBORN PHARAOHS

> Do not be afraid. Stand firm and you will see the deliverance the LORD will bring you today. The Egyptians you see today *you will never see again.*
>
> —EXODUS 14:13, NIV, EMPHASIS ADDED

Pharaoh is the type of the devil. He was stubborn. He kept hardening his heart. He kept changing his mind. No matter how much judgment came, he kept hardening his heart. But finally God had one thing to break him—he took his firstborn. Pharaoh still came after them, but God said, "Don't worry about him; I am going to drown him in the sea, and you will see him no more!"

I pray that every pharaoh, every stubborn pharaoh, be drowned and you will not see him again! You may have to go on a fast not one time; you may have to fast ten times. It took ten plagues to break Pharaoh's power. It's time to break those stubborn pharaohs. Sometimes a pharaoh may be a person— controlling devil, witch, warlock, Jezebel, a person who wants to control your life, your church.

I hate to use this example, but it is what comes to my mind. In *The Wizard of Oz* when the Wicked Witch of the East threatened the other one, the latter laughed and said, "Ha, ha, ha! Rubbish. You have no power here!" In the same way, you need to laugh at the devil. When the devil threatens you, just laugh, "Ha, ha, ha! Rubbish. You have no power here!" I watch that movie just to see that. I know that's one witch talking to another, but just eliminate the witch part, and you'll get it.

Don't let those demon spirits threaten you! I don't care if they are flying around the room on a broom with a black hat on. Declare: "No witch, no warlock, and no Jezebel will control my life. I am a servant of Jesus Christ, and whom the Son sets free is free indeed. No apostle, no doctor apostle, no bishop, no archbishop, no archbishop deluxe...I don't care what your title is...no prophet, no prophetess, whatever, you are not called to control my life. You are not called to dominate me and manipulate me and intimidate me. The devil is a liar!"

Sometimes it takes more than one judgment, battle, or victory to break stubborn enemies. There is something about stubborn enemies. You can hit them one time, but they keep coming back. It seemed that no matter what God did to loosen Pharaoh's grip on the children of Israel, he would not let God's people go. Even Pharaoh's advisors told him, "This is the finger of God. You cannot fight God." (See Exodus 8:19.) And eventually even he had to bow his knee to the King of kings.

It is time to put a hurting on the devil. We are not going to leave them alone, even as they cry out, "Let us alone" (Mark 1:23–24, KJV). We are going to put pressure on them. We are going to bind, rebuke, cast out, pray, fast, and deal with the powers of hell. They have been left alone for too long. Nobody was praying, fasting, taking authority, or preaching. They have had full sway in the generations. They did what they wanted to do. But now there is a new breed being raised up. There are pastors, prophets, apostles, teachers, evangelists, and everyday believers who will not leave the enemy alone until he is gone!

NEVER AGAIN CONFESSIONS

Never again will Pharaoh (Satan) control me, because I have been delivered from his power.

Never again will I allow the devil to do what he desires in my life, but I resist the devil, and he flees from me (James 4:7).

Never again will I listen to or believe the lies of the devil, for he is a liar and the father of lies (John 8:44).

Never again will I be vexed by unclean spirits (Luke 6:18).

Never again will I be harassed by the enemy (Matt. 9:36, AMP).

Never again will I be bound, for Christ has made me free. I am free indeed (John 8:36).

Never again will I allow the demons of double-mindedness to confuse me and make me indecisive (James 1:8).

Never again will I allow curses to hinder my life. I break every curse, for I have been redeemed from the curse (Gal. 3:13).

Never again will I open the door for demons to come into my life through unforgiveness (Matt. 18:35).

Never again will I open the door for demons to enter my life through habitual sin.

Never again will I open the door for demons to enter my life through occult involvement.

Never again will I open the door for demons to enter through rebellion and disobedience.

Never again will the demon of mind control affect my thinking.

I sever all the tentacles of mind control.

Never again will serpent and scorpion spirits affect my life, for I have power to tread on serpents and scorpions.

Never again will the enemy be my master; Jesus is my Lord.

Never again will I tolerate the works of the devil in my life, for Jesus came and destroyed the works of the devil (1 John 3:8).

Never again will I compromise my standards and holiness; the Word of God is my standard, not the standards of the world (2 Cor. 10:2, NIV).

Never again will I allow the enemy to control any part of my life, but my life is under the control of the Spirit and Word of God.

Never again will I allow the enemy to control my destiny, but God is the revealer and finisher of my destiny.

Never again will I allow the enemy to abort any plan of God for my life.

Never again will I allow people to draw me away from the love of God, but I commit myself to walking in love, for God is love (1 John 4:7–8).

Never again will I shut up my bowels of compassion (1 John 3:17, KJV).

Never again will I behave unseemly, for love does not behave unseemly (1 Cor. 13:5, KJV).

Never again will I be easily provoked, for love is not easily provoked (1 Cor. 13:5).

Never again will I seek my own, for love does not seek its own (1 Cor. 13:5).

Never again will I think evil, for love does not think evil (1 Cor. 13:6).

Never again will I lose hope, for love hopes all things (1 Cor. 13:7).

Never again will I give up, for love endures all things (1 Cor. 13:7).

Never again will I allow the accuser to accuse me, for I am washed and cleansed by the blood of the Lamb (Rev. 1:5; 7:14).

Never again will I allow sorrow and sadness to control my soul, for the Lord has taken away my sorrow and pain (Isa. 65:19).

Never again will the heavens be shut over my life, but the Lord has opened the windows of heaven (Mal. 3:10).

Chapter 5

FASTING TO OVERCOME
THE SPIRIT OF FEAR

For God has not given us the spirit of fear, but of power, and love, and self-control.

—2 TIMOTHY 1:7

FEAR IS A paralyzing spirit that keeps people bound in many areas of their lives. This spirit manifests itself in numerous ways: fear of rejection (works with rejection and self-rejection), fear of abandonment, fear of hurt, fear of authority (including pastors), fear of witchcraft, fear of career, fear of dying, fear of failure, fear of the future, fear of responsibility, fear of darkness, fear of being alone, fear of what people think of you, fear of what people say about you, fear of hell, fear of demons and deliverance, fear of poverty, fear of germs, fear of darkness, fear of marriage, fear of dogs, fear of accidents, fear of man, fear of Jezebel, fear of confrontation, fear of poverty, and more.

There are also extreme fears such as panic, panic attacks, terror, fright, apprehension, sudden fear, and more. Talkativeness, nervousness, worry, anxiety, and tension can also be part of the fear cluster of demons all related to rejection.

All of these manifestations must be broken in the name of Jesus.

FASTING BREAKS THE POWER OF FEAR

Do not be afraid, land; exult and rejoice, for the LORD has done great things!

—JOEL 2:21

Do you desire to see great things happen in your life and in your family? The Lord desires to do great things for His covenant people. Fasting will break the spirit of fear in your life and in your family's life and will prepare the way for great things to happen. These great things include signs and wonders.

PRAY

In the name of Jesus, I loose myself from all fears including childhood fears, fears from trauma, fears from the past, and all inherited fears. Amen.

DECLARATIONS FOR DELIVERANCE FROM REJECTION

I declare that You have sanctified me with Your word; Your word over me is truth (John 17:17).

Lord, You are my light and my salvation. You are the strength of my life. I will not fear anything or anyone (Ps. 27:1).

I believe and receive what You have said about me.

Your truth sets me free from the spirit of rejection.

You have nailed my rejection to the cross. I am set free.

You were despised and rejected. You are acquainted with my grief and sorrow. But by Your stripes, I am healed of rejection (Isa. 53:3–5).

The Lord is with me. I will not be afraid. What can man do to me (Ps. 118:6)?

The lines have fallen to me in pleasant places; yes, I have a good inheritance (Ps. 16:6).

I am blessed with all spiritual blessings in heavenly places in Christ (Eph. 1:3).

I have been chosen by God from the foundation of the world (Eph. 1:4).

I am holy and without blame (Eph. 1:4).

I have been adopted as Your child according to the good pleasure of Your will (Eph. 1:5).

I am accepted in the Beloved (Eph. 1:6).

I am redeemed through the blood of Jesus (Eph. 1:7).

I am an heir (Eph. 1:11).

I am seated in heavenly places in Christ Jesus (Eph. 2:6).

I am the workmanship of the Lord, created in Christ Jesus for good works (Eph. 2:10).

I am a fellow citizen with the saints and members of the household of God (Eph. 2:19).

I have been given exceedingly great and precious promises, that I may be a partaker of the divine nature of Christ (2 Pet. 1:4).

My inner man is strengthened with might by the Spirit of God (Eph. 3:16).

I am rooted and grounded in love (Eph. 3:17).

I am renewed in the spirit of my mind (Eph. 4:23).

I walk in love (Eph. 5:2).

I am filled with the Spirit of God (Eph. 5:18).

I am more than a conqueror (Rom. 8:37).

I am an overcomer by the blood of the Lamb (Rev. 12:11).

I am the righteousness of God in Christ Jesus (2 Cor. 5:21).

I am healed (1 Pet. 2:24).

The Son has set me free (John 8:36).

I am born of God; therefore, I am victorious (1 John 5:4).

PRAYERS FOR DIVINE SAFETY AND PROTECTION

Let the angel of the Lord encamp around me and protect me (Ps. 34:7).

Hold me up, and I will be safe (Ps. 119:117).

The name of Jesus is a strong tower. I run into it, and I am safe (Prov. 18:10).

Lord, You make me to dwell in safety (Ps. 4:8).

Set me in safety from them who puff at me (Ps. 12:5).

Let me dwell in my land safely (Lev. 26:5).

Lead me safely, and I will not fear. Let the sea overwhelm my enemies (Ps. 78:53).

Let me lie down and rest in safety (Job 11:18; Isa. 14:30).

I will dwell in safety; nothing shall make me afraid (Ezek. 34:28).

Keep me as the apple of Your eye, and hide me under the shadow of Your wings (Ps. 17:8).

I will trust in the covering of Your wings (Ps. 61:4).

In the shadow of Your wings will I trust (Ps. 57:1).

Be my covering from the storm and the rain (Isa. 4:6).

Be my covering from the wind and the tempest (Isa. 32:2).

Cover my head in the day of battle (Ps. 140:7).

Cover me with the shadow of Your hand (Isa. 51:16).

Cover me with Your feathers (Ps. 91:4).

Be my defense and refuge (Ps. 59:16).

Defend and deliver me (Isa. 31:5).

Let Your glory be my defense (Isa. 4:5).

Defend me from those who rise up against me (Ps. 59:1).

Lord, You are my shield and my hiding place (Ps. 119:114).

Lord, surround me with Your shield of protection (Ps. 5:12).

Bring them down, O Lord, my shield (Ps. 59:11).

Let Your truth be my shield (Ps. 91:4).

Lord, You are my sun and shield (Ps. 84:11).

Lord, You are my shield and exceeding great reward (Gen. 15:1).

I will not be afraid of ten thousand that have set themselves against me, because You are a shield for me (Ps. 3:1–6).

You are a strong tower from the enemy (Ps. 61:3).

Chapter 6

FASTING TO OVERCOME UNBELIEF AND DOUBT

And He did not do many mighty works there because of their unbelief.

—MATTHEW 13:58

And Jesus said unto them, Because of your unbelief: for verily I say unto you, If ye have faith as a grain of mustard seed, ye shall say unto this mountain, Remove hence to yonder place; and it shall remove; and nothing shall be impossible unto you.

—MATTHEW 17:20, KJV

U NBELIEF IS AN enemy to operating in the miraculous. Jesus could not operate in the power of God because of the unbelief of the people. The disciples could not cast out a strong demon because of unbelief. It is important to drive unbelief from your life. And one of the ways this is accomplished is through prayer and fasting. Prayer and fasting help us clear obstacles to our faith and faith-filled actions. During the healing revival of 1948–1957 many came into a healing ministry this way. Franklin Hall wrote a key book, *The Atomic Power With God With Prayer and Fasting.* He called fasting "supercharged prayer." He said the flesh had three primary needs or desires (food, sex, and status), and of these the need for food is dominant.

These natural desires are valid, but they can easily become too strong (inordinate desires equal lusts) and dominate us. Thus fasting is the way to assert control on the flesh where it counts. Fasting, coupled with prayer, is one of the most powerful weapons to break through and overcome unbelief. Jesus preceded

His ministry with fasting and returned in the power of the Spirit into Galilee. Jesus did not struggle with unbelief, and He operated in faith throughout His ministry. When challenged with unbelief in any situation, I encourage you to fast and pray for breakthrough.

PRAYERS THAT RELEASE SPECIAL FAITH

I will forsake any bondage that seeks to entrap me, looking forward by faith and setting my eyes on Him who is invisible (Heb. 11:27).

I decree and declare that by faith I will walk through my trials on dry ground, and my enemies will be drowned (Heb. 11:29).

I will encircle the immovable walls in my life, and by my faith those walls will fall down (Heb. 11:30).

I will subdue kingdoms, rain down righteousness, obtain promises, and stop the mouths of lions because of my faith (Heb. 11:33).

I am established and anointed by God (2 Cor. 1:21).

I activate my mustard seed of faith and say to this mountain of sickness and disease in my life, "Be removed and go to another place." Nothing will be impossible to me (Matt. 17:20).

I declare that I have uncommon, great faith in the power of Jesus Christ, faith that cannot be found anywhere else (Matt. 8:10).

I pray as Your anointed disciples prayed, "Increase my faith!" (Luke 17:5).

I will not stagger at the promise of God through unbelief, but I will stand strong in the faith, giving glory to God (Rom. 4:20).

My faith increases the more I hear, and hear by the Word of God (Rom. 10:17).

I walk by faith and not by sight (2 Cor. 5:7).

I declare that I feel the substance and see the evidence of the things that I have faith for (Heb. 11:1).

I see through the eyes of faith the promise of things afar off. I am persuaded of their reality. I embrace them, knowing that I am a stranger and pilgrim on this earth (Heb. 11:13).

I will stand firm and not waver. I will come boldly before God, asking in faith (James 1:6).

I will not suffer shipwreck in my life, because I have faith and a good conscience (1 Tim. 1:19).

I declare that my faith works together with my works, and by my works my faith is made perfect (James 2:22).

I will show my faith by the works I do (James 2:18).

Because of my faith in Jesus I have boldness and confident access to approach God (Eph. 3:12).

I am a son of Abraham because I have faith (Gal. 3:7).

I am a son of God because I have faith in Christ Jesus (Gal. 3:26).

I go in peace because my faith has saved me (Luke 7:50).

My faith is alive (James 2:17).

The Spirit of God has given me the gift of faith (1 Cor. 12:9).

I have faith in God (Mark 11:22).

Let it be to me according to my faith (Matt. 9:29).

No man has dominion over my faith. I stand by faith (2 Cor. 1:24).

Like Stephen, I do great wonders and signs because I am full of faith (Acts 6:8).

My faith is not in the wisdom of men but in the power of God (1 Cor. 2:5).

I will not be sluggish. I will imitate those who through faith and patience inherit the promises of God (Heb. 6:12).

The just shall live by faith (Rom. 1:17).

The righteousness of God is revealed to me through faith in Jesus (Rom. 3:22).

I am justified by my faith in Jesus (Rom. 3:26).

I have access by faith to the grace of God (Rom. 5:2).

I am raised to life through faith in Christ (Col. 2:12).

By faith I receive the promise of God in my life (Gal. 3:22).

My faith and hope are in God (1 Pet. 1:21).

My faith will not fail (Luke 22:32).

By faith the promise of God is sure to me, the seed of Abraham (Rom. 4:16).

I pray the prayer of faith and will see the sick saved and raised up (James 5:15).

I take the shield of faith and quench all the fiery darts of the wicked one (Eph. 6:16).

I put on the breastplate of faith and love (1 Thess. 5:8).

I obtain for myself good standing and great boldness in my faith in Christ Jesus (1 Tim. 3:13).

Chapter 7

FASTING TO BREAK THE SPIRIT OF POVERTY

Blow the ram's horn in Zion, consecrate a fast, call a sacred assembly. . . . Then the LORD became jealous for His land and took pity upon His people. So the LORD answered and said to His people, Here! I am sending you grain, new wine, and oil, and you will be satisfied, and I will never again make you a disgrace among the nations. . . . Then the threshing floors will be filled with grain, and the vats will overflow with new wine and oil. And I will compensate you for the years the locusts have eaten.

—JOEL 2:15, 18–19, 24–25

T HERE ARE BELIEVERS who give. They believe God. They feel so bad because they can't seem to get a financial breakthrough. They can't seem to get employment or opportunities for their business. They can't seem to overcome, and they get depressed. They begin to feel as though they don't have enough faith, maybe they don't believe God enough, or maybe they're not saved like someone else, maybe they aren't close to God, maybe God doesn't like them, maybe God doesn't favor them the way He favors others. It could be a stubborn spirit of poverty that's been in their family for generations—a curse or a generational spirit—and that thing just will not let go. But I believe that with God nothing is impossible. It may be time to fast and pray until breakthrough comes.

In the Book of Joel, the prophet gave the people the proper response to the locust invasion that can help believers today as they seek deliverance in the area of their finances. Locusts represent demons that devour. Locusts represent the spirits of poverty and lack. The locusts had come upon Israel and devoured the harvest. Joel encouraged the people to fast and repent. God promised to hear their prayers and answer by sending corn, wine, and oil.

Corn, wine, and oil represent prosperity. Fasting breaks the spirit of poverty and releases the spirit of prosperity. I have seen countless numbers of believers struggle in the area of their finances. Prosperity is elusive to many. This is because the demons of poverty have not been bound through fasting and prayer.

In Deuteronomy 8:3, 7–9, 18 God allowed the people to hunger in the wilderness by feeding them with only manna. They ate manna for forty years. This preceded their entering the Promised Land. Fasting helps prepare a believer for the good land. This is a land without scarceness. This is a land with no lack. Fasting humbles the soul (Ps. 35:13). God rewards those who fast (Matt. 6:18). Tremendous blessings are released for those who understand the power of fasting and do it.

Fasting is one of the ways we can break generational strongholds of poverty. Fasting prepares a believer for prosperity by bringing him or her into a place of humility. God has promised to exalt the humble (1 Pet. 5:6). Financial promotion is part of this exaltation. God gives grace (favor) to the humble (James 4:6). Favor is a part of financial prosperity. Fasting releases grace and favor upon a person's life. This will break the cycle of poverty and failure.

PRAYERS FOR PROSPERITY AND FINANCIAL RELEASE

I break all assignments of the enemy against my finances in the name of Jesus.

I break all curses of poverty, lack, debt, and failure in the name of Jesus.

I seek first the kingdom of God and His righteousness, and all things are added unto me (Matt. 6:33).

I rebuke and cast out all spirits of the cankerworm, palmerworm, caterpillar, and locust that would eat up my blessings in the name of Jesus (Joel 2:25).

Lord, teach me to profit, and lead me in the way I should go (Isa. 48:17).

You are Jehovah-Jireh, my provider (Gen. 22:14).

You are El Shaddai, the God of more than enough.

Wealth and riches are in my house because I fear You and delight greatly in Your commandments (Ps. 112:1–3).

The blessing of the Lord upon my life makes me rich.

I am blessed coming in and blessed going out.

I am God's servant, and He takes pleasure in my prosperity (Ps. 35:27).

Jesus, You became poor, that through Your poverty I might be rich (2 Cor. 8:9).

I meditate on the Word day and night, and whatever I do prospers (Ps. 1:3).

Let peace be within my walls and prosperity within my palace (Ps. 122:7).

I am Your servant, Lord. Prosper me (Neh. 1:11).

The God of heaven will prosper me (Neh. 2:20).

I live in the prosperity of the King (Jer. 23:5).

Through Your favor I will be a prosperous person (Gen. 39:2).

Lord, You have called me, and You will make my way prosperous (Isa. 48:15).

Lord, release the wealth of the wicked into my hands (Prov. 13:22).

Lord, bring me into a wealthy place (Ps. 66:12).

I give, and it is given to me—good measure, pressed down, shaken together, and running over (Luke 6:38).

Open the floodgates of heaven over my life, and I receive more than I have enough room to receive (Mal. 3:10).

Let every hole in my bag be closed in the name of Jesus (Hag. 1:6).

Rebuke the devourer for my sake (Mal. 3:11).

Let Your showers of blessing come upon my life (Ezek. 34:26).

Let my vats overflow (Joel 2:24).

Let my barns be filled with plenty and my presses burst with new wine (Prov. 3:10).

Command Your blessing upon my storehouse (Deut. 28:8).

Let my barns be full and overflowing. Let my sheep bring forth thousands and ten thousands. Let my oxen be strong to labor (Ps. 144:13–14).

Bring me into a good land without scarceness and lack (Deut. 8:9).

Chapter 8

FASTING TO BREAK CYCLES OF FAILURE AND DEFEAT

What agreement has Christ with Belial?

—2 CORINTHIANS 6:15

Christ has redeemed us from the curse of the law by being made a curse for us—as it is written, "Cursed is everyone who hangs on a tree."

—GALATIANS 3:13

DO FAILURE AND frustration seem to be your lot in life? Is your life characterized by continual setbacks and misfortune? Does it appear as though no matter what you do in life, you cannot seem to obtain the blessings of the Lord?

Often the most frustrating thing about this whole scenario is the fact that you are a believer and love the Lord. According to Galatians 3:13, we are redeemed from the curse. In other words, Jesus became a curse in our stead. If this is true, then how can a believer still be under a curse?

Unfortunately, there are still many believers living under curses even though they have been legally redeemed from curses. Just as a believer may have to fight a good fight of faith for healing, he or she may also have to fight a good fight of faith against curses. Many of the curses that can affect a person's life come as a result of one of the most wicked and vile spirits in the kingdom of darkness—the spirit of *Belial*.

He is a ruling spirit of wickedness. There is a host of demons that operate under his command, cursing the lives of people. When I observe the practices and sins that are happening in our nation today, I know that the spirit of Belial is behind them. Belial is a strongman in America as well as other nations of the world. Belial is a world ruler of wickedness. Jesus taught us the necessity of binding the strongman in order to spoil his goods (Matt. 12:29).

The prayers in this chapter are meant to do just that—as you pray, Belial, the world ruler of wickedness, will be bound, and his demonic hold on you and on your family and community will be broken. First, let's discuss what fasting does when it accompanies this kind of prayer.

Fasting causes you to become more fruitful. (See Joel 2:22.)

Fasting increases the fruit of a believer's life. This includes the fruit of the Spirit. God desires His people to be more fruitful. Fasting helps our ministries, businesses, and careers become more fruitful.

Fasting releases the rain. (See Joel 2:23.)

Rain represents the outpouring of the Holy Spirit. Rain also represents blessing and refreshing. Israel needed the former rain to moisten the ground for planting. They needed the latter rain to bring the crops to maturity. God has promised to give the former and latter rains in response to fasting.

Fasting moistens the ground (the heart) for the planting of the seed (the Word of God). Fasting causes the rain to fall in dry places. If you have not experienced revival in your spirit for a long time, through fasting the Lord can cause the rain of revival to fall in your life so that you can be refreshed and renewed.

Fasting breaks limitations, releases favor, and brings enlargement. (See Esther 4:14–16.)

Fasting was a part of defeating the plans of Haman to destroy the Jews. The whole nation of Israel was delivered because of fasting. Esther needed favor from the king and received it as a result of fasting. Fasting releases favor and brings great deliverance. The Jews not only defeated their enemies but they were also enlarged. Mordecai was promoted, and Haman was hung.

Enlargement comes through fasting. Fasting breaks limitations and gives you more room to expand and grow. God desires to enlarge our borders (Deut. 12:20). God wants us to have more territory. This includes natural and spiritual territory. Fasting breaks limitations and causes expansion.

Fasting will cause you to have great victory against overwhelming odds. (See 2 Chronicles 20:3.)

Jehoshaphat was facing the combined armies of Moab, Ammon, and Edom. He was facing overwhelming odds. Fasting helped him to defeat these enemies. Fasting helps us to have victory in the midst of defeat.

Jehoshaphat called a fast because he was afraid. Fear is another stronghold that many believers have difficulty overcoming. Fasting will break the power of the demon of fear. Spirits of terror, panic, fright, apprehension, and timidity can be overcome through fasting. Freedom from fear is a requirement to live a victorious lifestyle.

PRAYERS FOR BLESSING AND FAVOR

Lord, bless me and keep me. Make Your face to shine upon me, and be gracious unto me. Lord, lift up Your countenance upon me and give me peace (Num. 6:24–26).

Make me as Ephraim and Manasseh (Gen. 48:20).

Let me be satisfied with favor and filled with Your blessing (Deut. 33:23).

Lord, command Your blessing upon my life.

Give me revelation, and let me be blessed (Matt. 16:17).

I am the seed of Abraham through Jesus Christ, and I receive the blessing of Abraham. Lord, in blessing, bless me, and in multiplying, multiply me as the stars of heaven and as the sand of the seashore.

Let Your showers of blessing be upon my life (Ezek. 34:26).

Turn every curse sent my way into a blessing (Neh. 13:2).

Let Your blessing make me rich (Prov. 10:22).

Let all nations call me blessed (Mal. 3:12).

Let all generations call me blessed (Luke 1:48).

I am a son of the blessed (Mark 14:61).

I live in the kingdom of the blessed (Mark 11:10).

My sins are forgiven, and I am blessed (Rom. 4:7).

Lord, You daily load me with benefits (Ps. 68:19).

I am chosen by God, and I am blessed (Ps. 65:4).

My seed is blessed (Ps. 37:26).

Let me inherit the land (Ps. 37:22).

I am a part of a holy nation, and I am blessed (Ps. 33:12).

Lord, bless my latter end more than my beginning (Job 42:12).

Lord, let Your presence bless my life (2 Sam. 6:11).

I drink the cup of blessing (1 Cor. 10:16).

Lord, bless me, and cause Your face to shine upon me, that Your way may be known upon the earth and Your saving health among all nations. Let my land yield increase, and let the ends of the earth fear You (Ps. 67).

I know You favor me because my enemies do not triumph over me (Ps. 41:11).

Lord, be favorable unto my land (Ps. 85:1).

Lord, grant me life and favor (Job 10:12).

In Your favor, Lord, make my mountain stand strong (Ps. 30:7).

Lord, I entreat Your favor (Ps. 45:12).

Let Your favor cause my horn to be exalted (Ps. 89:17).

Lord, this is my set time for favor (Ps. 102:13).

Remember me, O Lord, with the favor that You bring unto Your children, and visit me with Your salvation (Ps. 106:4).

Lord, I entreat Your favor with my whole heart (Ps. 119:58).

Let Your favor be upon my life as a cloud of the latter rain (Prov. 16:15).

Let Your beauty be upon my life, and let me be well favored (Gen. 29:17).

I am highly favored (Luke 1:28).

Lord, let me receive extraordinary favor.

PRAYERS FOR ENLARGEMENT AND INCREASE

Break off of my life any limitations and restrictions placed on my life by any evil spirits in the name of Jesus.

I bind and cast out all python and constrictor spirits in the name of Jesus.

Bless me indeed, and enlarge my coast. Let Your hand be with me, and keep me from evil (1 Chron. 4:10).

Cast out my enemies, and enlarge my borders (Exod. 34:24).

Lord, You have promised to enlarge my borders (Deut. 12:20).

Enlarge my heart so I can run the way of Your commandments (Ps. 119:32).

My mouth is enlarged over my enemies (1 Sam. 2:1).

Enlarge my steps so I can receive Your wealth and prosperity (Isa. 60:5–9).

I receive deliverance and enlargement for my life (Esther 4:14).

The Lord shall increase me more and more, me and my children (Ps. 115:14).

Let Your kingdom and government increase in my life (Isa. 9:7).

Let me increase in the knowledge of God (Col. 2:19).

O Lord, bless me and increase me (Isa. 51:2).

Let me increase exceedingly (Gen. 30:43).

Let me increase with the increase of God (Col. 2:19).

Let me increase and abound in love (1 Thess. 3:12).

Increase my greatness, and comfort me on every side (Ps. 71:21).

Let me increase in wisdom and stature (Luke 2:52).

Let me increase in strength and confound the adversaries (Acts 9:22).

Let Your grace and favor increase in my life.

Let the years of my life be increased (Prov. 9:11).

Let the Word of God increase in my life (Acts 6:7).

Bless me in all my increase (Deut. 14:22).

Let my giving and tithes increase (Deut. 14:22).

Chapter 9

FASTING TO BREAK THE SPIRITS OF PROCRASTINATION, PASSIVITY, AND SLOTHFULNESS

Slothfulness gradually prevails over the faithful unless it be corrected.[1]

—JEAN CALVIN

J ESUS KNEW AT an early age that He must be about His Father's business. Some people always dream about tomorrow without ever doing anything today. What you do today will determine whether you will have success tomorrow. Success comes as a result of action.

Procrastinators are full of excuses. You must eliminate every excuse that stops you from doing what you have been called to do. Moses's excuse was his speech. Jeremiah's was his youth. There is no excuse worth stopping your movement toward success in God. God's grace is sufficient. Winners don't allow excuses to stop them from winning.

PROCRASTINATION AND INDECISION

Indecision results in procrastination, compromise, confusion, forgetfulness, and indifference. Indecision is one of the most debilitating problems in life because life is based on decisions. Indifference is an attitude that causes a person to avoid making decisions.

Procrastination is another way of avoiding a decision by just putting it off for a future time. It can also be rooted in the fear of making a decision. Our choices pave the way for success or failure. A double-minded person has a difficult time making decisions and often changes after making one. This results in wavering and always questioning a decision. Proper decision making is the result of wisdom and a stable personality.

PASSIVITY AND SLOTHFULNESS

Some people are too passive and lazy to maintain a successful and victorious life. Successful people are doers of the Word (James 1:22). I have often taught on the danger of passivity.

Passivity causes listlessness and lethargy, continual sadness, crying, defeatism, dejection, despair, despondency, discouragement, escapism, fatigue, gloom, gluttony, grief, guilt, heartache, heartbreak, hopelessness, hurt, hyperactivity, indifference, inner hurts, insomnia, laziness, lethargy, listlessness, loneliness, mourning, negativity, passivity, rejection, self-pity, sorrow, and tiredness. Many times, a person fighting passivity will feel like they are in a "funk," like they are going nowhere. Passivity immobilizes a person. Passivity results in withdrawal and lethargy. It takes away the natural desire to be aggressive in life. Passive people will not pursue and go after what they need to succeed in life. Passive people will let others do it for them.

Slothfulness is apathy, dullness, idleness, indolence, languor, laziness, lethargy, lifelessness, listlessness, passivity, slowness, sluggishness, tiredness. Slothfulness is an aversion to work or exertion. A slothful person has the characteristics of a sloth. A sloth is a slow-moving and stationary animal.

Slothfulness will put you in bondage. "The hand of the diligent shall bear rule: but the slothful shall be under tribute" (Prov. 12:24, KJV).

The sluggard is entangled. The way of the sluggard is painful. "The way of the sluggard is overgrown with thorns [it pricks, lacerates, and entangles him], but the way of the righteous is plain and raised like a highway" (Prov. 15:19, AMP).

Slothfulness opens the door for poverty. "Slothfulness casteth into a deep sleep; and an idle soul shall suffer hunger" (Prov. 19:15, KJV).

Slothfulness can open you up to death. "The desire of the slothful kills him, for his hands refuse to labor" (Prov. 21:25).

Slothfulness will cause your life to fall apart. Slothfulness leads to decay. "I went by the field of the slothful, and by the vineyard of the man void of understanding; and, lo, it was all grown over with thorns, and nettles had covered the face thereof, and the stone wall thereof was broken down" (Prov. 24:30–31, KJV). Then Ecclesiastes 10:18 says, "The roof beams sink in with slothfulness, and with the idleness of one's hands the house drips."

If we want to experience the full provision of the covenant operating in our lives, then we cannot be slothful and passive. There are pieces to the puzzle that require work. We must not be slow to act when God is telling us to move. We are commanded in Romans 12:11 not to be slothful in business but to be "fervent in spirit, [and to] serve the Lord."

PRAYERS FOR BOLDNESS AND COURAGE

I am bold as a lion (Prov. 28:1).

I have boldness and access with confidence by faith in Christ (Eph. 3:12).

I have much boldness in Christ (Philem. 1:8).

I have boldness to enter the holy place by the blood of Jesus (Heb. 10:19).

Lord, grant me the boldness that I may speak forth (Acts 4:29).

Lord, I pray with all prayers and supplication that I may open my mouth boldly to make known the mysteries of the gospel (Eph. 6:19).

Let me be much more bold to speak the Word without fear (Phil. 1:14).

I have great boldness in the faith of Christ Jesus (1 Tim. 3:13).

I come boldly to the throne of grace, that I may obtain mercy, and find grace to help in time of need (Heb. 4:16).

I boldly say, "The Lord is my helper, and I will not fear what man will do to me" (Heb. 13:6).

I have boldness in the day of judgment: because as He is, so am I in this world (1 John 4:17).

Let men see my boldness and know that I have been with Jesus (Acts 4:13).

Let me be filled with the Holy Ghost that I may speak the word of God with boldness (Acts 4:31).

I will wait on the Lord and be of good courage and He will strengthen my heart (Ps. 27:14).

I will be strong and courageous; I will not be afraid, for the Lord is with me wherever I go (Josh. 1:9).

I will be courageous to keep and do all that the Lord has told me (Josh. 23:6).

I will deal courageously and the Lord will be with me (2 Chron. 19:11).

Chapter 10

FASTING FOR HEALING FROM INFIRMITY

Then your light shall break forth as the morning, and your healing shall spring forth quickly, and your righteousness shall go before you; the glory of the LORD shall be your reward.

—ISAIAH 58:8

ASTING WILL BREAK the power of sickness and infirmity and release healing in your life (Isa. 58:5–6, 8). Many believers struggle with sicknesses such as cancer, diabetes, high blood pressure, sinus problems, and chronic pain. These spirits of infirmity are often generational. Fasting helps eliminate chronic sickness and diseases. God has promised that our health will spring forth speedily.

According to Isaiah 58:8, you will be healed when you fast, but better yet, fasting can also serve as preventative medicine. The Bible says, "The glory of the LORD shall be your rear guard" (NKJV). In other words, sickness can't sneak up on you. God has your back. While everyone else is getting swine flu, you will be healthy. While it is said that there's no cure for the common cold, you will sail through cold season with not so much as one symptom, sniffle, or cough.

PRAYERS FOR HEALTH AND HEALING

I will live and not die, and I will proclaim the name of the Lord (Ps. 118:17).

Lord, You heal all of my diseases (Ps. 103:3).

57

Heal me, O Lord, and I will be healed (Jer. 17:14).

Jesus, arise over my life with healing in Your wings (Mal. 4:2).

I prosper and walk in health even as my soul prospers (3 John 2).

I am healed by the stripes of Jesus (Isa. 53:5).

Jesus carried my sickness and infirmities (Matt. 8:17).

I cast out all spirits of infirmity that would attack my body in the name of Jesus.

I break, rebuke, and cast out any spirit of cancer that would attempt to establish itself in my lungs, bones, breast, throat, back, spine, liver, kidneys, pancreas, skin, or stomach in the name of Jesus.

I rebuke and cast out all spirits causing diabetes, high blood pressure, low blood pressure, heart attack, stroke, kidney failure, leukemia, blood disease, breathing problems, arthritis, lupus, Alzheimer's, or insomnia in the name of Jesus.

I speak healing and strength to my bones, muscles, joints, organs, head, eyes, throat, glands, blood, marrow, lungs, kidneys, liver, spleen, spine, pancreas, eyes, bladder, ears, nose, sinuses, mouth, tongue, and feet in the name of Jesus.

I loose myself from all heart attacks rooted in fear, and I command all spirits of fear to leave in Jesus's name (Luke 21:26).

I loose myself from all cancer rooted in bitterness, unforgiveness, resentment, and slander of the tongue, and I command these spirits to come out in the name of Jesus.

I loose myself from lupus rooted in self-rejection, self-hatred, and guilt, and I cast these spirits out in the name of Jesus.

I loose myself from all multiple sclerosis rooted in self-hatred, guilt, and rejection from the father, and I cast these spirits out in the name of Jesus.

I loose myself from rheumatoid arthritis that is rooted in self-hatred and low self-esteem, and I command these spirits to come out in the name of Jesus.

I loose myself from high cholesterol that is rooted in anger and hostility and command these spirits to come out in the name of Jesus.

I loose myself from all sinus problems rooted in fear and anxiety, and I command these spirits to come out in the name of Jesus.

I loose myself from all high blood pressure rooted in fear and anxiety, and I command these spirits to come out in the name of Jesus.

I loose myself from asthma rooted in fear concerning relationships in the name of Jesus.

I loose myself from a weakened immune system that is rooted in a broken spirit or broken heart, and I command these spirits to come out in the name of Jesus.

I loose myself from all strokes rooted in self-rejection, self-bitterness, and self-hatred, and I command these spirits to come out in the name of Jesus.

I loose myself from all bone diseases rooted in envy and jealousy, and I command these spirits to come out in the name of Jesus (Prov. 14:30).

Forgive me, Lord, for allowing any fear, guilt, self-rejection, self-hatred, unforgiveness, bitterness, sin, pride, or rebellion to open the door to any sickness or infirmity. I renounce these things in the name of Jesus.

Chapter 11

FASTING FOR DELIVERANCE FROM BITTERNESS, ANGER, AND UNFORGIVENESS

... watching diligently so that no one falls short of the grace of God, lest any root of bitterness spring up to cause trouble, and many become defiled by it.

—HEBREWS 12:15

Let all bitterness, wrath, anger, outbursts, and blasphemies, with all malice, be taken away from you. And be kind one to another, tenderhearted, forgiving one another, just as God in Christ also forgave you.

—EPHESIANS 4:31–32

BITTERNESS IS OFTEN the result of rejection and hurt. People become angry and bitter when they fail to forgive and release people who have wounded and offended them. Everyone has experienced some sort of pain in life, and many do not resolve it and, therefore, end up becoming bitter.

The root of bitterness has related spirits, including unforgiveness, rage, anger, violence, revenge, retaliation, and even murder. The Hebrew word for "bitterness," *marah*, connects bitterness and rebellion. *Marah* means to be (cause, make) bitter (or unpleasant); to rebel (or resist, cause to provoke); bitter, change, be disobedient, disobey, grievously, provocation, provoke (ing), (be) rebel (against, -lious).[1] Bitterness is repressed anger and is connected to stubbornness (refusal to forgive). The rejected person often has a hard time forgiving. Rejection hurts and creates offense, which requires forgiveness. Unforgiveness can breed bitterness. It is a vicious cycle.

Bitterness is a deep-rooted spirit. It goes deep into a person's emotions and is hard to dislodge because the person "feels" angry and other deep emotions that are so real to them. This demon gets rooted down into the flesh. Reacting in anger or revisiting the bitterness satisfies the flesh. But it is a pseudo satisfaction. It only causes harm to the flesh in the form of opening doors to spirits of infirmity, including arthritis and cancer. It is symbolized by gall and wormwood. This is why the root of bitterness needs to be broken through fasting, which starves the flesh. Bitterness is very common, and multitudes need deliverance from it.

Anger is a related spirit that stems from bitterness. It can be a stubborn demon. Some people just can't seem to overcome anger. They erupt, but feel so guilty.

Unforgiveness opens the door for tormenting spirits (Matt. 18). Unforgiveness is the result of being hurt, rejected, abandoned, disappointed, abused, raped, molested, taken advantage of, lied on, cheated, talked about, etc.

All of these spirits come as a result of rejection, which can prevent one from giving or receiving love from God or from other people. There is also a spirit called "rejection from the womb" that enters the womb because the child was unwanted. Self-rejection and fear of rejection are other related spirits. Rejection is also a doorkeeper. This spirit opens the door for other spirits to enter, including fear, hurt, unforgiveness, and bitterness. It links with rebellion, causing double-mindedness (see my book *Unshakeable* for more on this topic).

Almost everyone has experienced rejection at one time or another in life. People can be rejected because of their gender, skin color, economic status, size, shape, etc. Rejection is a major stronghold in the lives of many. But you can begin to attack all of the spirits connected with rejection, anger, bitterness, and unforgiveness through prayer and obedience. If things seem to not be shaking loose, add fasting to your prayer and watch God deliver you.

PRAYERS TO RELEASE YOU FROM ANGER

I will cease from anger and put away wrath to stay connected to God. If I wait on Him, I will inherit the earth (Ps. 37:8–9).

My whole body is sick, and my health is broken because of my sins. But I confess my sins and am deeply sorry for what I have done. Do not abandon me, O Lord. Come quickly to help me, O Lord my Savior (Ps. 38:3, 18, 22, NLT).

I will speak soft words, kind words, and words of life to turn wrath and anger away from me. I will not grieve anyone with my words (Prov. 15:1).

I will appease the strife against my health and my family by being slow to anger (Prov. 15:18).

I am better than the mighty because I control my anger. There is more gain in ruling my spirit than conquering a city (Prov. 16:32).

I use discretion to defer my anger; I earn esteem by overlooking wrongs (Prov. 19:11).

I will not sin against my own soul by provoking the King to anger (Prov. 20:2).

I will silence anger with a secret gift (Prov. 21:14).

I declare that anger's reign in my life will come to an end (Prov. 22:8).

I cast out the cruelty and destruction of wrath and anger. They will not flood my emotions any longer (Prov. 27:4).

I will be slow to anger and will keep its clutches from resting in my bosom (Eccles. 7:9).

Let all wrath and anger be put away from me (Eph. 4:31).

I am a new person, having been renewed after the image of Him who created me; therefore, I put off anger (Col. 3:8–10).

I will not discourage my children by provoking them to anger (Col. 3:21).

PRAYERS TO FREE YOU FROM BITTERNESS

Lord, I give the bitterness of my soul to You. Please look upon my affliction and remember me. I will go in peace because You have granted my petition (1 Sam. 1:10–11, 17).

I will speak openly to You, O Lord, and release all of my bitterness to You (Job 7:11).

I will speak to You, God, in the bitterness of my soul. I will find the root of why my spirit contends with Yours (Job 10:1–2).

I declare that I will not die in the bitterness of my soul, and I will eat with pleasure (Job 21:25).

My heart knows its own bitterness (Prov. 14:10); I release it to You.

I will raise wise children who will cause me no grief or bitterness (Prov. 17:25).

I had great bitterness, but in love You delivered me from the pit of corruption. For You have put all my sins behind Your back (Isa. 38:17).

I was in bitterness and in the heat of my spirit, but the hand of the Lord is strong upon me (Ezek. 3:14).

I repent of my wickedness and pray to God that the thoughts of my heart be forgiven, for I am bound by bitterness and iniquity (Acts 8:21–23).

My mouth is full of cursing and bitterness, but You have shown me a better way and I have been made right in Your sight (Rom. 3:14, 21–22).

I diligently look within myself so that I will not be defiled by any root of bitterness that may spring up (Heb. 12:15).

PRAYERS TO FREE YOU FROM UNFORGIVENESS

I will go to my brother and ask that he forgive me of my trespasses against him (Gen. 50:17).

I pray that my brother will forgive me so that when I go before God, He will take this death away from me (Exod. 10:17).

Like Moses, I come to You asking Your forgiveness on behalf of Your people and myself. Thank You, God, that You forgive all those who sin against You, for You have blotted them out of Your book (Exod. 32:32–33).

God, I thank You that when You hear our prayers You also forgive us (1 Kings 8:30).

You have heard from heaven, forgiven my sin, and have delivered me into the land You promised my fathers (1 Kings 8:34).

You have heard from heaven, forgiven my sin, and have taught me the good way in which I should walk (1 Kings 8:36).

You have heard from heaven, forgiven my sin, and will do and give me according to my ways because You know my heart (1 Kings 8:39).

Forgive me of my sins, and have compassion upon me (1 Kings 8:50).

I am called by Your name and have humbled myself before You.

I pray and seek Your face and have turned from my wicked ways. Now You will hear from heaven and forgive my sin and heal me (2 Chron. 7:14).

Look upon my affliction and my pain, and forgive all my sins (Ps. 25:18).

You, O Lord, are good and ready to forgive. Your mercy is plentiful to all those who call on You (Ps. 86:5).

The Lord declares that He will forgive my iniquity and remember my sin no more (Jer. 31:34).

O Lord, hear. O Lord, forgive. O Lord, listen and do! For I am called by Your name (Dan. 9:19).

As I forgive others, Lord, I pray that You will forgive me (Matt. 6:12).

I will forgive those who have wronged me, because if I don't, God will not forgive me (Matt. 6:14–15).

You have healed me and said, "Arise and take up your bed," so that I will know that You have the power to forgive sins on Earth (Matt. 9:6).

Like the servant who owed the king ten thousand talents, I too have been forgiven much. Therefore I will go and forgive all those who have sinned against me so that I will not be given over to the tormentors (Matt. 18:23–35).

I will forgive any person with whom I ought, so that when I stand praying, my Father in heaven will forgive me also (Mark 11:25).

Chapter 12

FASTING FOR VICTORY OVER ANXIETY AND DEPRESSION

Now may the God of hope fill you with all joy and peace in believing, so that you may abound in hope, through the power of the Holy Spirit.

—ROMANS 15:13

I N THE BIBLE sadness and depression are related to a spirit of heaviness. Manifestations of this spirit include despondency, despair, discouragement, and hopelessness. There are multitudes of people who suffer from bouts of depression. Many of them are being medicated. Going in and out of depression is a sign of double-mindedness. This also includes withdrawal and isolation. Depression is at an all-time high. There are many people being treated for manic depression (bipolar). This can even drive people to hopelessness and suicide. Depression can cause a person to desire to escape, which can lead to sleepiness and abusing alcohol and drugs.

Fasting will cause the joy and the presence of the Lord to return to your life (Mark 2:20). The presence of the bridegroom causes joy. Weddings are filled with joy and celebration. When a believer loses joy and the presence of the Lord, he or she needs to fast. Fasting causes the joy and presence of the Lord to return. No believer can live a victorious life without the presence of the Bridegroom. The joy of the Lord is our strength (Neh. 8:10).

THE GUT AND DEPRESSION

I have studied the subject of fasting, and I have also studied the belly (gut). Since fasting is connected with the belly, gut, and the stomach, there must be something about fasting that affects our gut in a positive way.

In Scripture the belly can be consumed with grief, and can be a symbol of defeat and shame. We know the belly can be affected by stress, anxiety, and worry. I have also learned that we often lay hands on a person's stomach when doing deliverance. Spirits of fear and lust often reside in this area as well.

> Have mercy upon me, O LORD, for I am in trouble: mine eye is consumed with grief, yea, my soul and my *belly*.
> —PSALM 31:9, KJV, EMPHASIS ADDED

> For our soul is bowed down to the dust: our *belly* cleaveth unto the earth.
> —PSALM 44:25, KJV, EMPHASIS ADDED

The connection between the digestive system and the central nervous system, consisting of the brain and the spinal cord, is well known. Here's what Harvard Medical School said about the gut-brain connection:

> Have you ever had a "gut-wrenching" experience? Do certain situations make you "feel nauseous"? Have you ever felt "butterflies" in your stomach? We use these expressions for a reason. The gastrointestinal tract is sensitive to emotion. Anger, anxiety, sadness, elation —all of these feelings (and others) can trigger symptoms in the gut.
>
> The brain has a direct effect on the stomach. For example, the very thought of eating can release the stomach's juices before food gets there. This connection goes

both ways. A troubled intestine can send signals to the brain, just as a troubled brain can send signals to the gut. Therefore, a person's stomach or intestinal distress can be the cause or the product of anxiety, stress, or depression. That's because the brain and the gastrointestinal (GI) system are intimately connected—so intimately that they should be viewed as one system.[1]

"Have you ever had that familiar feeling of 'butterflies' in the stomach?" *Scientific American* asks. "Underlying this sensation is an often-overlooked network of neurons lining our guts that is so extensive some scientists have nicknamed it our 'second brain.'"

> A deeper understanding of this mass of neural tissue, filled with important neurotransmitters, is revealing that it does much more than merely handle digestion or inflict the occasional nervous pang. The little brain in our innards, in connection with the big one in our skulls, partly determines our mental state and plays key roles in certain diseases throughout the body.[2]

I believe fasting helps our gut, and in turn helps our emotions and brain. Fasting will help you think clearer and help you overcome depression, sadness, grief, confusion, stress, worry, and anxiety.

LOOSE YOUR EMOTIONS

Are you loosed in your emotions? The emotions are a part of the soul along with the will and the mind. There are many people bound and blocked in their emotions. Spirits of hurt, rejection, anger, broken heart, grief, sadness, hatred, bitterness, and rage can occupy the emotions, causing emotional pain.

Your emotions were created by God to express joy and sorrow. Both should be natural responses to different situations. The enemy, however, comes in to cause extremes in the emotional realm and even blockage whereby a person is unable to express the proper emotions. Emotional pain and bondage can come as a result of traumatic experiences of the past, including rape, incest, abuse, death of a loved one, war, tragedies, rejection, abandonment, accidents, etc.

You can be free from unchecked, unpredictable, and fluctuating emotions. Ask the Lord to bring you balance and self-control in this area. Let's pray.

> *In the name of the Lord Jesus Christ, by the authority given to me to bind and loose, I loose my emotions from every evil spirit that has come in as a result of experiences of the past. I loose myself from all hurt, deep hurt, pain, sadness, grief, anger, hatred, rage, bitterness, fear, and bound and blocked emotions. I command these spirits to come out, and I decree freedom to my emotions in the name of the Lord Jesus Christ. Amen.*

PRAYERS THAT DESTROY OPPRESSION

I rebuke and cast out any spirit that would attempt to oppress me in the name of Jesus.

Jesus, You went about doing good and healing all those oppressed of the devil (Acts 10:38).

I strip all power from spirits that would oppress me (Eccles. 4:1).

I rebuke and cast out all spirits of poverty that would oppress me (Eccles. 5:8).

I rebuke all spirits of madness and confusion that would attempt to oppress my mind in the name of Jesus (Eccles. 7:7).

O Lord, undertake for me against all my oppressors (Isa. 38:14).

Lord, You are my refuge from the oppressor (Ps. 9:9).

Deliver me from the wicked that would oppress me and from my deadly enemies that would surround me (Ps. 17:9).

Deliver me from oppressors that seek after my soul (Ps. 54:3).

Break in pieces the oppressor (Ps. 72:4).

I rebuke and cast out all spirits of affliction, sorrow, and anything attempting to bring me low in the name of Jesus (Ps. 107:39).

Leave me not to my oppressors (Ps. 119:121).

Let not the proud oppress me (Ps. 119:122).

Deliver me from the oppression of men (Ps. 119:134).

I rule over my oppressors (Ps. 14:2).

Let the oppressors be consumed out of the land (Isa. 16:4).

I rebuke the voice of the oppressor in the name of Jesus (Ps. 55:3).

I am established in righteousness, and I am far from oppression (Isa. 54:14).

Punish those who attempt to oppress me (Jer. 30:20).

The enemy will not take my inheritance through oppression (Ezek. 46:18).

Execute judgment against my oppressors (Ps. 146:7).

PEACE CONFESSIONS

My life is good and my days are good because I keep my tongue from evil.

I hate evil, I do good, and I seek after peace.

I commit my life to peace and prosperity.

I will live in peace, I will walk in peace, and I will seek peace.

Jesus is my peace.

Jesus is my Jehovah Shalom, my prosperity and my peace.

I will walk in peace all the days of my life.

I will see good, I will love life, and I will have many good days.

I am blessed and prosperous, because I am a peaceable person.

Chapter 13

FASTING FOR FREEDOM FROM GUILT

The faith that you have, have as your own conviction before God.
Happy is he who does not condemn himself in what he approves.

—ROMANS 14:22

G UILT IS ONE of the worst things you can allow to control your life. Guilt comes from condemnation, shame, unworthiness, embarrassment, low self-esteem, and feelings of inferiority (low class, bottom of the barrel, always last place, insecure, never good enough). Guilt is the root of countless diseases and unhappiness. There are people who live their lives feeling guilty about things they did years ago. They have never forgiven themselves for something they did or did not do. They literally punish themselves. They feel unworthy, ashamed, and embarrassed, which often turns into self-rejection.

Guilt is a terrible demon, and you have to be delivered from it. You can ask God to forgive you, and you can ask the people you may have hurt to forgive you, but the most important thing you need to do is forgive yourself. This is the hardest part for many people. They believe God forgives them and other people forgive them, but they can't forgive themselves.

We have all done things that we are not proud of, but we must remember that when we've done all we can do to make things right, Jesus is our righteousness. He covers us. If we don't get this into our spirits, then we are open to being afflicted by many sicknesses and diseases, because there is a connection between the spirit, soul, and body. The Bible says, "I pray that in all respects you may prosper and be in good health, just as your soul prospers" (3 John 1:2, NAS). Your soul is your mind, will, and emotions. If your soul is not healthy and you are overcome with hurt, shame, guilt, fear, and rejection, your body will eventually be affected. It doesn't always happen overnight.

The longer you carry these things, the more damage they do.

LOOSE YOUR CONSCIENCE

To be *loosed* means to be forgiven and pardoned. You have been forgiven by the Father through the blood of Jesus. You are loosed from guilt, shame, and condemnation. You must also be loosed from the law (legalism).

The law brings condemnation and judgment, but Jesus brings forgiveness and reconciliation. We loose our conscience by applying the blood of Jesus, by faith. Satan uses guilt and condemnation to beat down the believers. Believers who don't understand grace are struggling in their Christian lives, never measuring up to religious standards imposed upon them through legalism. To be free in your conscience is to have peace in your mind. The peace of God rules in your heart.

In the name of Jesus, I loose myself from all guilt, shame, condemnation, self-condemnation, and legalism. Amen.

PRAYERS AGAINST GUILT AND CONDEMNATION

I rebuke and cast out all spirits of guilt, shame, and condemnation through the blood of Jesus.

I bind and cast out all spirits of unworthiness in the name of Jesus.

I loose myself from all diabetes rooted in rejection, self-hatred, inheritance, and guilt, and I command these spirits to come out in the name of Jesus.

I loose myself from lupus rooted in self-rejection, self-hatred, and guilt, and I cast these spirits out in the name of Jesus.

I loose myself from all multiple sclerosis rooted in self-hatred, guilt, and rejection from the father, and I cast these spirits out in the name of Jesus.

Forgive me, Lord, for allowing any fear, guilt, self-rejection, self-hatred, unforgiveness, bitterness, sin, pride, or rebellion to open the door to any sickness or infirmity. I renounce these things in the name of Jesus.

DESTROYING YOKES AND REMOVING BURDENS

I remove all false burdens placed on me by people, leaders, or churches in the name of Jesus (1 Thess. 2:6).

I remove all heavy burdens placed on my life by the enemy in the name of Jesus.

Let your anointing break the enemy's burden from off my neck, and let every yoke be destroyed (Isa. 10:27).

Remove my shoulder from every burden (Ps. 81:6).

I cast my cares upon the Lord (1 Pet. 5:7).

I cast my burdens upon the Lord, and He sustains me (Ps. 55:22).

Lord, break the yoke of the enemy's burden, and break the staff and the rod of the oppressor as in the day of Midian (Isa. 9:4).

Let every yoke of poverty be destroyed in the name of Jesus.

Let every yoke of sickness be destroyed in the name of Jesus.

Let every yoke of bondage be destroyed in the name of Jesus (Gal. 5:1).

Let every unequal yoke be broken in the name of Jesus (2 Cor. 6:14).

I destroy every yoke and burden of religion and legalism placed on my life by religious leaders in the name of Jesus (Matt. 23:4).

Let every burdensome stone be released from my life in the name of Jesus (Zech. 12:3).

I take upon my life the yoke and burden of Jesus (Matt. 11:30).

Chapter 14

FASTING TO BREAK FREE FROM A PAINFUL PAST

This one thing I do, forgetting those things which are behind and reaching forward to those things which are ahead, I press toward the goal to the prize of the high calling of God in Christ Jesus.

—PHILIPPIANS 3:13–14

I HAVE MINISTERED TO many believers who are still bound and tied to their past. The past can be a chain that keeps you from enjoying the present and being successful in the future. While ministering deliverance to a young man, I encountered a strong spirit dwelling in him who boasted that he would not depart. I commanded the spirit to identify himself, and he replied that his name was Past. The spirit proceeded to explain that it was his job to keep the young man bound to his past so that he could not be successful in his Christian walk. The young man had been through a divorce, and his past continued to haunt him. This encounter helped to give me a revelation of the fact that there are numerous spirits assigned to people to keep them bound to the past that has left scars and wounds that have not completely healed. Many of these wounds have been infected and have become the dwelling places of unclean spirits.

People need to be loosed not only from demons but also from other people. Ungodly soul ties are avenues that spirits of control and manipulation utilize when working upon their unwary victims.

Let's look at some of the things that could cause spirits to attach themselves to people who have had traumatic experiences in their past. For the purposes of clarity, we find the word *trauma* defined by Webster's as "a disordered psychic or behavioral state resulting from severe mental or emotional stress or physical injury."[1]

Traumatic experiences can open the door for demons. These can and often include accidents. Mentioned below are two such traumatic experiences that greatly affect the lives of individuals.

1. Rape

> They have raped the women in Zion, the virgins in the towns of Judah.
>
> —Lamentations 5:11, jb

Rape is one of the most traumatic experiences a person can have. It is a violation that leaves deep scars in the psyche of the person who is victimized by this ungodly act. The door is opened for a host of evil spirits to enter and operate throughout the life of the victim.

Spirits of hurt, distrust, lust, perversion, anger, hatred, rage, bitterness, shame, guilt, and fear can enter and torment the person for the rest of their life if not discerned and cast out. Rape can also be a curse, and there is often a history of this sin in the bloodline.

Rape has always been in the history of oppressed people. It was (and is) common for victors to rape the women of the vanquished. It is one of the most shameful and humiliating acts that can be perpetrated upon an oppressed people.

Often victims of rape carry sexual blockages into marriage, including spirits of frigidity, bound and blocked emotions, hatred of men, and fear of sexual intercourse. Individuals can grow up with deep roots of bitterness that poison the system, opening the door for spirits of sickness and infirmity, including cancer.

> *Father, in Jesus's name, I loose myself from this prowling demon that sought to steal, kill, and destroy my body, my sexuality, and my worth. I loose myself from any hatred, bitterness, and unforgiveness. I loose myself from blaming myself for this violation. I loose myself from any soul ties, spirits of infirmity, or other evil spirits that would seek to latch on to my life because of this trauma. I loose myself from any bondages that would keep me from experiencing healthy and free marital intimacy. Amen.*

2. Incest

Another common sexual violation is the sin of incest. Incest can also result from a curse, and there can be a history of this sin in the bloodline. It is an act that causes much shame and guilt. It opens the door for all kinds of curses, including insanity, death, destruction, confusion, perversion, and sickness. Often the victim blames himself for this act even though it may have been the result of a seducing spirit.

> *Father, in Jesus's name, I loose myself from the shame, guilt, soul ties, and any other hindering spirit that would try to keep me from living a whole and healthy life. I loose myself from the painful memories of this abuse and declare that I am washed clean, inside and out. I loose myself from every demonic spirit*

*that would seek to enter through this open door, and
I shut this door to my past and pray a hedge of protection around my future. Amen.*

LOOSE YOUR MEMORY

Forgetting those things which are behind…

—PHILIPPIANS 3:13

There is an evil spirit named memory recall that can cause a
person to have flashbacks of past experiences. This keeps a
person in bondage to traumatic experiences of the past. This
spirit causes a person to remember experiences of hurt, pain,
and rejection. Although there may be experiences in your life
you will never completely forget, you should not be in bondage
to the past through your memory.

The enemy should not be able to trigger things in your
memory that hinder you in your present or future life. This is
why your memory needs to be loosed from bad experiences of
hurt and trauma.

*Father, in Jesus's name, I loose myself from the
effects of all the bad memories, painful memories,
and memories of the past that would hinder me in
the present or future. Amen.*

DECLARATIONS THAT BREAK THE
GRIP OF A PAINFUL PAST

The days of my mourning have past. I have now found favor in the
sight of the King (Gen. 50:4).

My winter has past. The rain is over and gone. Flowers appear on the earth and the time of singing has come (Songs 2:11–12).

The mysteries of my past sufferings have been revealed to me. Now I can rejoice.

Glory forever to Jesus Christ who has established me according to the gospel and the preaching of Christ. My past is no longer a kept secret. Its purpose has been revealed through the prophetic Scriptures that I might believe and obey.

In my past I was not one of God's people, but now I am. I had not received His mercy, but now I have (1 Pet. 2:10).

There is hope for my future.

The Lord has plans to give me a peaceful and hopeful future (Jer. 29:11).

The sign of God's covenant is with me and all my future generations.

This one thing I will do: Forget the past and reach forward to the things that are ahead. I will press toward the goal of the prize of the high calling of God in Christ Jesus (Phil. 3:13–14).

Chapter 15

FASTING TO BREAK FREE FROM DRUG AND ALCOHOL ADDICTION

Do not be drunk with wine, for that is reckless living. But be filled with the Spirit.
—Ephesians 5:18

T HE SPIRIT OF addiction is rooted deeply in the flesh. I've dealt with people who just could not quit smoking. It's difficult for them to get delivered from just a smoking habit. They do everything to break it. They pray. They come for deliverance. They just can't break it. It's a stubborn spirit. Sometimes they get frustrated, and the enemy condemns them and tells them, "You're not strong." But sometimes you have to fast when you are trying to break free from a spirit of addiction, because it is so rooted in the flesh.

All addictions operate in similar ways—drugs, alcohol, gluttony, eating disorders, food addictions. They must be broken through fasting and prayer.

ADDICTION IS CONNECTED TO THE SPIRIT OF BELIAL

Now Hannah spoke in her heart; only her lips moved, but her voice was not heard. Therefore Eli thought she was drunk. So Eli said to her, "How long will you be drunk? Put your wine away from you!" And Hannah answered and said, "No, my lord, I am a woman of sorrowful spirit. I have drunk neither wine nor intoxicating drink, but have poured out my soul before the LORD. Do not consider your maidservant a wicked woman, for out of the abundance of my complaint and grief I have spoken until now."

—1 SAMUEL 1:13–16, NKJV

In the King James Version, verse 16 says, "Count not thine handmaid for a daughter of Belial." Eli had thought that Hannah was drunk. The spirit of Belial operates through alcohol and drunkenness. Drunkenness is a way to break down the morals and open people up to lust and perversion. I believe that spirits of alcohol and drunkenness operate under the strongman of Belial. It is a known fact that many children of alcoholic parents are often the victims of sexual abuse, including incest. Alcohol can also open the door for spirits of rape, including "date rape" (which is so prevalent on many college campuses).

Here are some prayers you can pray while fasting to help break the grip of these spirits off of your life.

PRAYERS AGAINST DRUNKENNESS

Father, help me to listen to the warning in Your Word to "take heed to yourselves, lest your hearts be weighed down with carousing, drunkenness, and cares of this life." Keep me focused on living for You, so that I am not caught in the devil's snare to cause me to be unprepared when "that Day come on you unexpectedly" (Luke 21:34, NKJV).

Father, help me to "live and conduct *[myself]* honorably and becomingly as in the [open light of] day, not in reveling (carousing) and drunkenness, not in immorality and debauchery (sensuality and licentiousness), not in quarreling and jealousy" (Rom. 13:13, AMP).

Lord, I want to do only what You want me to do, for following my own desires will lead me astray. "People's desires make them give in to immoral ways, filthy thoughts, and shameful deeds. They worship idols, practice witchcraft, hate others, and are hard to get along with. People become jealous, angry, and selfish. They not only argue and cause trouble, but they are envious. They get drunk, carry on at wild parties, and do other evil things as well" (Gal. 5:19–21, cev). I don't want to live like that, Lord. I want to honor and serve You in everything I do.

Father, You give good advice in Your Word—advice I want to follow: "Oh listen, dear child—become wise; point your life in the right direction. Don't drink too much wine and get drunk; don't eat too much food and get fat. Drunks and gluttons will end up on skid row, in a stupor and dressed in rags" (Prov. 23:21, The Message).

Father, Your Word warns me to be careful about the kind of people I hang around with. Help me to heed Your advice to "not associate with anyone who calls himself a brother but is sexually immoral or greedy, an idolater or a slanderer, a drunkard or a swindler" (1 Cor. 5:11, niv). Help me to choose my friends wisely.

Lord, I do not want to "be drunk with wine, for that is reckless living." I want to be "filled with the Spirit" (Eph. 5:18). Fill me with Your Spirit, Lord.

God, from the time of Aaron, You have instructed Your Christian leaders and ministers: "When you enter the Tent of Meeting, don't drink wine or strong drink, neither you nor your sons, lest you die. This is a fixed rule down through the generations. Distinguish between the holy and the common" (Lev. 10:8–10, The Message). May I never fail You by making what is holy common by my sinfulness and drunkenness.

Father, You taught that anyone who is "consecrating yourself totally to God" should not "drink any wine or beer, no intoxicating drink of any kind" (Num. 6:2, The Message). Help me to understand that drunkenness destroys my ability to stay consecrated to You, and help me to turn away from that which has the power to turn me away from You.

Lord, help me to follow the simple advice of Your Word, which says, "It isn't smart to get drunk! Drinking makes a fool of you and leads to fights" (Prov. 20:1, CEV).

Father, You have strong advice about the dangers of drunkenness for those who are called to be leaders, for in Your Word, You say, "Kings and leaders should not get drunk or even want to drink" (Prov. 31:4, CEV). Help me to honor Your Word in this matter.

PRAYERS AGAINST DRUG AND ALCOHOL ADDICTION

I command all spirits of addiction to come out of my appetite in the name of Jesus.

I renounce all addiction to drugs, alcohol, or any legal or illegal substance that has bound me in the name of Jesus.

I break all generational curses of pride, lust, perversion, rebellion, witchcraft, idolatry, poverty, rejection, fear, confusion, addiction, death, and destruction in the name of Jesus.

Chapter 16

FASTING FOR VICTORY OVER GLUTTONY AND OVERINDULGENCE

*Whose end is destruction, whose God is their belly, and whose glory
is in their shame—who set their mind on earthly things.*

—Philippians 3:19, nkjv

You don't want your belly to be your god. The belly is the center of your appetite. You cannot allow your appetite to control your life. In Philippians 3, Paul wrote of those whose God was their belly. They were earthly minded. They were carnal. In other words, they were rebellious gluttons.

Carnality will hinder your walk with God. Fasting helps you overcome carnality. Fasting helps you walk in the spiritual. Fasting is spiritual. Fasting is the opposite of being earthly and carnal (being controlled by your appetite).

Romans 16:18 says, "For such people do not serve our Lord Jesus Christ, but their own appetites, and through smooth talk and flattery they deceive the hearts of the unsuspecting."

One of the benefits of fasting is that it teaches us moderation. Moderate means being within reasonable limits; not excessive or extreme. Excess is detrimental. Food is stimulating. Our brains become quickly accustomed to stimuli, and the result is a lack of true satisfaction. Denying yourself food is denying one of the things that stimulate us the most in life.

> While at first our senses are acutely tuned in to the input they are receiving, they fast become acclimated to the stimuli.

The stimuli lose the ability to wow us and give us pleasure. We become numb to it. At this point most people reach for something new to experience those fresh feelings anew.

This is certainly the answer society gives us for our restlessness, our boredom, our anxiousness, and unhappiness. The answer is always MORE. More stimulation. More sex, more movies, more music, more drinking, more money, more freedom, more food. More of anything is sold as the cure for everything. Yet paradoxically, the more stimulation we receive, the less joy and enjoyment we get out of it. The key to experiencing greater fulfillment and pleasure is actually moderation.[1]

Moderation is important to satisfaction in life. We have lost the importance of moderation. Our society is filled with excess. Fasting is self-denial. Fasting is a powerful weapon against excess. Fasting helps us become temperate. Temperance is moderation and self-restraint, as in behavior or expression. Excess is lust and self-indulgence.

> For in earlier times of our lives it may have sufficed us to do what the Gentiles like to do, when we walked in immorality: lusts, drunkenness, carousing, debauchery, and abominable idolatries.
>
> —1 Peter 4:3

Excess is the opposite of the Spirit-filled life.

> Do not be drunk with wine, for that is reckless living. But be filled with the Spirit.
>
> —Ephesians 5:18

Gluttony and drunkenness are manifestations of excess and are connected to rebellion and stubbornness. Deuteronomy 21:20 says, "They shall say to the elders of his city, 'This son of ours is stubborn and rebellious. He will not listen to us. He is a glutton and a drunkard.'"

> They are surprised that you do not join them in the same excess of wild living, and so they speak evil of you.
>
> —1 PETER 4:4

DECLARATIONS FOR SELF-CONTROL AND SATISFACTION IN WHAT GOD PROVIDES

I am a lover of what is good. I am self-controlled. I am just. I am holy. I am temperate (Titus 1:8).

I am sober, serious, temperate, sound in faith, in love, in patience (Titus 2:2).

I inhabit the fruit of the Spirit of love, joy, peace, patience, gentleness, goodness, faith, meekness, and self-control; against such there is no law (Gal. 5:22–23)

I strive for the prize, therefore I exercise self-control in all things (1 Cor. 9:25).

God has not given me the spirit of fear, but of love, power, and self-control (2 Tim. 1:7).

I will be self-controlled in all things (2 Tim. 4:5).

I will feast at the appropriate time with self-control and not drunkenness (Eccles. 10:17).

I will be satisfied with the abundant bread of heaven (Ps. 105:40).

The Lord satisfies the longing of my soul and fills me with goodness (Ps. 107:9).

The Lord opens His hand and satisfies me (Ps. 145:16).

The Lord will abundantly bless my provision and satisfy me with bread (Ps. 132:15).

I will see the face of God in righteousness. I will be satisfied when I awake with His likeness (Ps. 17:15).

I will be meek so that I can eat and be satisfied (Ps. 22:26).

My soul will be satisfied as with marrow and fatness, and my mouth will praise the Lord with joyful lips (Ps. 63:5).

The Lord will satisfy me in the early morning with His mercy that I may rejoice and be glad all my days (Ps. 90:14).

The Lord satisfies my mouth with good things, so that my youth is renewed like the eagle's (Ps. 103:5).

I am righteous. I eat to the satisfying of my soul (Prov. 13:25).

I am like the good man. I will be satisfied with my ways (Prov. 14:14).

The Lord will feed me with the finest of wheat, and with honey out of the rock will He satisfy me (Ps. 81:16).

The fear of the Lord will tend to my life. Because I fear the Lord, I will live satisfied and will not be visited with evil (Prov. 19:23).

I will find satisfaction. I will be able to say, "It is enough" (Prov. 30:15).

He who loves money will not be satisfied with money; nor he who loves abundance with increase. This also is vanity (Eccles. 5:10). I will find my substance in God alone.

The Lord will satiate my soul with abundance and I will be satisfied with His goodness (Jer. 31:14).

Chapter 17

FASTING TO HEAR AND RECEIVE A WORD FROM THE LORD

And thou shalt remember all the way which the LORD *thy God led thee these forty years in the wilderness, to humble thee, and to prove thee, to know what was in thine heart, whether thou wouldest keep his commandments, or no. And he humbled thee, and suffered thee to hunger, and fed thee with manna, which thou knewest not, neither did thy fathers know; that he might make thee know that man doth not live by bread only, but by every word that proceedeth out of the mouth of the* LORD *doth man live. Thy raiment waxed not old upon thee, neither did thy foot swell, these forty years.*

—DEUTERONOMY 8:2–4, KJV

JESUS FASTED FORTY days in the wilderness. Israel was in the wilderness forty years. Jesus is the true Israel of God. Israel was allowed to hunger for forty years. God fed them with manna and suffered them to hunger, to humble them and teach them that man does not live by bread only, but by every word that proceeds out of the mouth of the Lord.

Fasting will bring greater humility to your life, and fasting will help you understand that you do not live by bread alone, but by every word that proceeds from the mouth of God. When you fast, you are saying, "I live by the word of God. The word of God is my strength. The Lord is the strength of my life."

The prophetic word is a proceeding word. Fasting puts us in a position to receive the proceeding word and live by the proceeding word. Fasting helps you release the proceeding word. God can put His word in your mouth to speak and release.

In the above verse, we read that their raiment did not wax old. Fasting helps us keep our raiment fresh and new. Raiment is a garment. Garments can wax old through religion and tradition. We also see in this passage that their feet did not swell. "Feet" represent your walk with the Lord, your spiritual growth and journey to maturity in Him, and your ability to hear His direction for your life and follow it. Fasting helps keep your walk from being hindered.

FASTING WILL RESULT IN ANSWERED PRAYER

> Then you shall call, and the LORD shall answer; you shall cry, and He shall say, Here I am.
>
> —ISAIAH 58:9

Demonic interference causes many prayers to be hindered. Daniel fasted twenty-one days to break through demonic resistance and receive answers to his prayers. (See Daniel 10.) The prince of Persia withstood the answers for twenty-one days. Daniel's fast helped an angel to break through and bring the answers.

Fasting will cause many answers to prayer to be accelerated. These include prayers for salvation of loved ones and deliverance. Fasting helps to break the frustration of unanswered prayer.

FASTING RELEASES DIVINE GUIDANCE

> And the LORD shall guide you continually, and satisfy your soul in drought, and strengthen your bones; and you shall be like a watered garden, and like a spring of water, whose waters do not fail.
>
> —ISAIAH 58:11

Many believers have difficulty making correct decisions concerning relationships, finances, and ministry. This causes setbacks and wasted time because of foolish decisions. Fasting will help believers make correct decisions by releasing divine guidance. Fasting eliminates confusion. Fasting causes clarity and releases understanding and wisdom to make correct decisions. Fasting is recommended for those who are making important decisions such as marriage and ministry choices.

PRAYERS FOR REVELATION

You are a God that reveals secrets. Lord, reveal Your secrets unto me (Dan. 2:28).

Reveal to me the secret and deep things (Dan. 2:22).

Let me understand things kept secret from the foundation of the world (Matt. 13:35).

Let the seals be broken from Your Word (Dan. 12:9).

Let me understand and have revelation of Your will and purpose for my life.

Give me the spirit of wisdom and revelation, and let the eyes of my understanding be enlightened (Eph. 1:17).

Let me understand heavenly things (John 3:12).

Open my eyes to behold wondrous things out of Your Word (Ps. 119:18).

Let me know and understand the mysteries of the kingdom (Mark 4:11).

Let me speak to others by revelation (1 Cor. 14:6).

Reveal Your secrets to Your servants the prophets (Amos 3:7).

Let the hidden things be made manifest (Mark 4:22).

Hide Your truths from the wise and prudent, and reveal them to babes (Matt. 11:25).

Let Your arm be revealed in my life (John 12:38).

Reveal the things that belong to me (Deut. 29:29).

Let Your Word be revealed unto me (1 Sam. 3:7).

Let Your glory be revealed in my life (Isa. 40:5).

Let Your righteousness be revealed in my life (Isa. 56:1).

Let me receive visions and revelations of the Lord (2 Cor. 12:1).

Let me receive an abundance of revelations (2 Cor. 12:7).

Let me be a good steward of Your revelations (1 Cor. 4:1).

Let me speak the mystery of Christ (Col. 4:3).

Let me receive and understand Your hidden wisdom (1 Cor. 2:7).

Hide not Your commandments from me (Ps. 119:19).

Let me speak the wisdom of God in a mystery (1 Cor. 2:7).

Let me make known the mystery of the gospel (Eph. 6:19).

Make known unto me the mystery of Your will (Eph. 1:9).

Open Your dark sayings upon the harp (Ps. 49:4).

Let me understand Your parables; the words of the wise and their dark sayings (Prov. 1:6, KJV).

Lord, lighten my candle and enlighten my darkness (Ps. 18:28).

Make darkness light before me (Isa. 42:16).

Give me the treasures of darkness and hidden riches in secret places (Isa. 45:3).

Let Your candle shine upon my head (Job 29:3).

My spirit is the candle of the Lord, searching all the inward parts of the belly (Prov. 20:27).

Let me understand the deep things of God (1 Cor. 2:10).

Let me understand Your deep thoughts (Ps. 92:5).

Let my eyes be enlightened with Your Word (Ps. 19:8).

My eyes are blessed to see (Luke 10:23).

Let all spiritual cataracts and scales be removed from my eyes (Acts 9:18).

Let me comprehend with all saints what is the breadth and length and depth and height of Your love (Eph. 3:18).

Let my reins instruct me in the night season, and let me awaken with revelation (Ps. 16:7).

Chapter 18

FASTING FOR DELIVERANCE FROM SEXUAL IMPURITY

Then all the children of Israel, and all the people, went up, and came unto the house of God, and wept, and sat there before the LORD, and fasted that day until even, and offered burnt offerings and peace offerings before the LORD . . . and [then] the LORD smote Benjamin before Israel.

—JUDGES 20:26, 35, KJV

S EXUAL SIN IS one of the hardest sins to break. Many believers struggle with generational lust that has passed down through the family lines. Lust spirits cause much shame, guilt, and condemnation. This robs the believer of the confidence and boldness he should have as a believer. Many believers struggle with masturbation, pornography, perversion, and fornication. Fasting will drive these generational spirits from your life.

In Judges 19:22 we read about some men in a city who wanted to have sexual relations with the guest of an old man in that city:

> While they were enjoying themselves, the men of the city, who were wicked men, surrounded the house and pounded on the door. They said to the old man, the master of the house, "Bring out the man who came to your house, so we can have relations with him."

They were homosexuals who were identified as sons of Belial. The man of the house tried to discourage them and offered them his daughter and the guest's concubine instead. The men took the concubine of the guest and abused her all night. The abuse was so severe that she died. (See Judges 19:25–30.) The guest then took a knife and cut the concubine into twelve pieces and sent them to every tribe in Israel. His concubine had been raped to death.

The men who raped the concubine were from the tribe of Benjamin. The men of Israel gathered against the city and requested they turn over the guilty men. The children of Benjamin would not listen and instead gathered themselves to battle. The children of Benjamin destroyed twenty-two thousand men of Israel on the first day (Judg. 20:21), and they destroyed eighteen thousand on the second day (v. 25).

In Judges 20:26–35, we see that Israel could not overcome Benjamin until they fasted. The resistance of Benjamin implies that there was something demonic behind them. Twelve tribes could not overcome one tribe because of this demonic resistance. This resistance was broken after fasting. This was the only way perversion was rooted out of the tribe of Benjamin. Fasting helps you break free from the chains of sexual perversion and lust.

Lust

Lust is a demonic substitute for true love. Rejected people will seek out relationships and often get involved in sexual immorality at a young age. The spirit of harlotry can manifest at a young age and can be seen in young women who dress provocatively.

Sexual impurity has become rampant in our society. Sexual lust spirits include adultery, fornication, whoredom, harlotry, seduction, sexual impurity, perversion, homosexuality, lesbianism, masturbation, pornography, incest, fantasy lust, sodomy, and uncleanness.

Lust is not only sexual but can also manifest in materialism, overindulgence, food addictions (gluttony, bulimia, anorexia, and extreme dieting), drug and alcohol addictions, clothing, and so on.

Perversion

The perversion cluster of demons can lead to homosexuality, lesbianism, fetishes, molestation, and other deviant sexual activities. Perversion can be a manifestation of self-rejection when people reject their own sexual identity. These are simply attempts to overcome rejection.

Loose Your Sexual Character

> Flee fornication.
>
> —1 Corinthians 6:18, kjv

The sex drive is one of the strongest appetites in the human body. Satan desires to control and pervert it outside the marital relationship in which it is blessed. Many believers struggle in this area with the companion spirits of guilt and condemnation. Spirits of lust and perversion can operate in any part of the physical body, including the genitals, hands, eyes, mouth, stomach, and so on. Any part of the body given to sexual sin will be invaded and controlled by spirits of lust. (An example would be the eyes in viewing pornography, the hands in acts of masturbation, or the tongue in filthy conversation.)

Sexual impurity is a strong-rooted spirit because it is rooted in the flesh. The longer a person has been in a lifestyle—homosexuality, adultery, masturbation—the more difficult it is. That thing will stubbornly cling to your flesh. Sometimes fasting is the way to weaken the root system because when you fast, you are dealing with the flesh. You are subduing your flesh. That's why demons hate fasting. They don't want you to fast. But if you truly want to be free, I recommend that you fast.

Begin your fast for deliverance from sexual impurity with this prayer:

> *In the name of Jesus, I loose all members of my body—*
> *including my mind, memory, eyes, ears, tongue,*
> *hands, feet, and my entire sexual character—from*
> *all lust, perversion, sexual impurity, uncleanness,*
> *lasciviousness, promiscuity, pornography, fornica-*
> *tion, homosexuality, fantasy, filthiness, burning pas-*
> *sion, and uncontrollable sex drive. Amen.*

DELIVERANCE AND RENUNCIATION OF SEXUAL SIN

I renounce all sexual sin that I have been involved with in the past, including fornication, masturbation, pornography, perversion, fantasy, and adultery in the name of Jesus.

I break all curses of adultery, perversion, fornication, lust, incest, rape, molestation, illegitimacy, harlotry, and polygamy in the name of Jesus.

I command all spirits of lust and perversion to come out of my stomach, genitals, eyes, mind, mouth, hands, and blood in the name of Jesus.

I present my body to the Lord as a living sacrifice (Rom. 12:1).

My members are the members of Christ. I will not let them be the members of a harlot (1 Cor. 6:15).

I release the fire of God to burn out all unclean lust from my life in the name of Jesus.

I break all ungodly soul ties with former lovers and sexual partners in the name of Jesus.

I cast out all spirits of loneliness that would drive me to ungodly sexual relationships in the name of Jesus.

I command all spirits of hereditary lusts from my ancestors to come out in the name of Jesus.

I command all spirits of witchcraft that work with lust to leave in the name of Jesus.

I take authority over my thoughts and bind all spirits of fantasy and lustful thinking in the name of Jesus.

I cast out all marriage-breaking spirits of lust that would break covenant in the name of Jesus.

I cast out and loose myself from any spirit spouses and spirits of incubus and succubus in the name of Jesus.

I cast out all spirits of perversion, including Moabite and Ammonite spirits of lust, in the name of Jesus.

I receive the spirit of holiness in my life to walk in sexual purity in the name of Jesus (Rom. 1:4).

I loose myself from the spirit of the world, the lust of the flesh, the lust of the eyes, and the pride of life. I overcome the world through the power of the Holy Spirit (1 John 2:16).

I am crucified with Christ. I mortify my members. I do not let sin reign in my body, and I will not obey its lust (Rom. 6:6–12).

Chapter 19

FASTING TO BREAK GENERATIONAL CURSES

Those from among you shall rebuild the old waste places; you shall raise up the foundations of many generations; and you shall be called, the Repairer of the Breach, the Restorer of Paths in which to Dwell.

—Isaiah 58:12

MANY OF THE obstacles believers encounter are generational. Generational curses result from the iniquity of the fathers. Generational sins such as pride, rebellion, idolatry, witchcraft, occult involvement, Masonry, and lust open the door for evil spirits to operate in families through generations. Demons of destruction, failure, poverty, infirmity, lust, and addiction are major strongholds in the lives of millions of people.

LOOSE THYSELF FROM EVIL INHERITANCE

Weaknesses and tendencies can be inherited from the sins of the fathers. For example, a person born to alcoholic parents will have a higher chance of becoming an alcoholic. Sicknesses and diseases can run in the bloodline, which is why doctors will often check to see if there is a history of certain sicknesses in the family. Some of these evil inheritances include lust, perversion, witchcraft, pride, rebellion, divorce, alcohol, hatred, bitterness, idolatry, poverty, ignorance, and sicknesses (including heart disease, cancer, diabetes, and high blood pressure).

Familiar spirits are demons familiar with a person and the family because often they have been in the family for generations. Sometimes these spirits are difficult to break because of how deep their roots run into the family line.

But this kind can come out through prayer combined with fasting. Fasting helps loose the bands of wickedness. Fasting lets the oppressed go free. Fasting helps us to rebuild the old waste places. Fasting reverses the desolation that results from sin and rebellion. Begin with this prayer:

> *In the name of Jesus, I loose myself from all evil inheritance, including inherited weaknesses, attitudes, thought patterns, sickness, witchcraft, lust, rebellion, poverty, ungodly lifestyles, and strife. Amen.*

PRAYERS TO CAST OUT GENERATIONAL SPIRITS

I am redeemed from the curse of the law (Gal. 3:13).

I break all generational curses of pride, lust, perversion, rebellion, witchcraft, idolatry, poverty, rejection, fear, confusion, addiction, death, and destruction in the name of Jesus.

I command all generational spirits that came into my life during conception, in the womb, in the birth canal, and through the umbilical cord to come out in the name of Jesus.

I break all spoken curses and negative words that I have spoken over my life in the name of Jesus.

I break all spoken curses and negative words spoken over my life by others, including those in authority, in the name of Jesus.

I command all ancestral spirits of freemasonry, idolatry, witchcraft, false religion, polygamy, lust, and perversion to come out of my life in the name of Jesus.

I command all hereditary spirits of lust, rejection, fear, sickness, infirmity, disease, anger, hatred, confusion, failure, and poverty to come out of my life in the name of Jesus.

I break the legal rights of all generational spirits operating behind a curse in the name of Jesus. You have no legal right to operate in my life.

I bind and rebuke all familiar spirits and spirit guides that would try to operate in my life from my ancestors in the name of Jesus.

I renounce all false beliefs and philosophies inherited by my ancestors in the name of Jesus.

I break all curses on my finances from any ancestors that cheated or mishandled money in the name of Jesus.

I break all curses of sickness and disease and command all inherited sickness to leave my body in the name of Jesus.

Through Jesus, my family is blessed (Gen. 12:3).

I renounce all pride inherited from my ancestors in the name of Jesus.

I break all oaths, vows, and pacts made with the devil by my ancestors in the name of Jesus.

I break all curses by agents of Satan spoken against my life in secret in the name of Jesus (Ps. 10:7).

I break all written curses that would affect my life in the name of Jesus (2 Chron. 34:24).

I break every time-released curse that would activate in my life as I grow older in the name of Jesus.

I break every curse Balaam hired against my life in the name of Jesus (Neh. 13:2).

Chapter 20

FASTING TO BREAK THE POWER OF WITCHCRAFT, MIND CONTROL, AND UNGODLY SOUL TIES

Regard not them that have familiar spirits, neither seek after
wizards, to be defiled by them: I am the LORD your God.

—LEVITICUS 19:31, KJV

WITCHCRAFT MANIFESTS IN different ways including sorcery, divination, intimidation, control, and manipulation. Saul and Jezebel are biblical examples of those who used witchcraft to gain what they desired.

> The demon of witchcraft can also work in many other kinds of relationships. A pastor may seek to control members of his staff or his entire congregation. A business executive may intimidate his subordinates....People who habitually use manipulation or intimidation to control others open themselves to the bondage and influence of a demon of witchcraft. If this happens, they will be unable to relate to anyone apart from these tactics. It will be no longer just the flesh at work, but a supernatural power that can bring whomever they control into a condition of spiritual slavery.[1]

The whole realm of the occult falls under the umbrella of witchcraft. This includes false religions, fortune-telling, new age, ESP, astrology, hypnosis, Eastern religions, masonry, telepathy, palmistry, etc. These are all manifestations of rebellion side of the double-minded personality. I talk about double-mindedness in my book *Unshakeable*.

THE CURSE OF UNGODLY SOUL TIES AND GODLESSNESS

> Do not be unequally yoked together with unbelievers. For what fellowship has righteousness with unrighteousness? What agreement has Christ with Belial? Or what part has he who believes with an unbeliever?
> —2 CORINTHIANS 6:14–15

When there is an unequal yoke between believers and unbelievers, we call this an ungodly soul tie. Breaking ungodly soul ties is a key to deliverance. Ungodly association causes evil spirits to be transferred. If Belial cannot directly control you, he will influence you through ungodly association. (Read more about the spirit of Belial in my book *Prayers That Break Curses*.)

Associating with the wrong people can cause you to receive an evil transfer of spirits. One of the keys to being delivered from Belial's control is to break every ungodly soul tie and to obey the Word of God, which says, "Do not be unequally yoked together with unbelievers" (2 Cor. 6:14). The Amplified Bible says, "Do not be unequally yoked with unbelievers [do not make mismated alliances with them or come under a different yoke with them, inconsistent with your faith]."

This is the only time the name Belial is mentioned in the New Testament. I believe the Spirit of God chose this word to bring revelation to a spirit that the church must not in any way be in fellowship with. Verse 15 ties Belial with unrighteousness, darkness, infidels, and idolatry. The first reference to Belial in the Word of God ties him to idolatry. The Corinthians had been saved from a lifestyle of idolatry.

I believe that Belial is an end-time spirit who will be an enemy of the church. We are to separate ourselves from all uncleanness and filthiness that is associated with this ruling spirit.

The church at Corinth also had a problem with carnality. There were strife, envy, contention, sexual impurity, and even drunkenness taking place within the church. The Apostle Paul wrote the letter to Corinth to correct these problems and to set things in order.

LOOSE THYSELF FROM UNGODLY SOUL TIES

> Cursed be their anger, for it is fierce; and their wrath, for it is cruel: I will divide them in Jacob, and scatter them in Israel.
>
> —GENESIS 49:7

The Lord separated Simeon and Levi because they exerted a bad influence upon one another. A soul tie is a bond between two individuals; the souls (minds, wills, emotions) of individuals knit or joined together. Ungodly soul ties can be formed through fornication (Gen. 34:2–3) and witchcraft (Gal. 3:1; 4:17).

As mentioned earlier, people need to be loosed not only from demons but also from other people. Ungodly soul ties are avenues through which spirits of control, domination, witchcraft, and manipulation operate. If you are linked with the wrong people, you will be in bondage, often unknowingly.

It is never the will of God for one individual to control another. True freedom is being delivered from any controlling power that hinders you from fulfilling the will of God. Often those under control are unaware that they are being controlled. This is why many times the control is so difficult to break.

An ungodly soul tie will result in the presence of an evil influence in your life. While good soul ties help you in your walk with God, ungodly soul ties hinder you in your walk with the Lord. Ungodly soul ties in the Bible include 1) Ahab and Jezebel (1 Kings 18); 2) Solomon and his wives—they turned his heart away from the Lord (1 Kings 11:1–4); and 3) Levi and Simeon (Gen. 49:5–7).

Pray:

> *Father, in Jesus's name, I loose myself from all relationships that are not ordained of God, all relationships that are not of the Spirit but of the flesh, all relationship based on control, domination, or manipulation, and all relationships based on lust and deception. Amen.*

LOOSE THYSELF FROM OCCULT BONDAGE

The word *occult* means hidden. Involvement in the occult opens the door for many demons, including spirits of depression, suicide, death, destruction, sickness, mental illness, addiction, lust, etc. Occult practices include:

- Ouija board
- Horoscopes
- Palm reading
- Psychic
- Readers and advisers
- Drugs (from Greek word pharmakeia—sorcery)
- Tea leaf reading
- Black magic
- White magic
- ESP

Pray:

> *Father, in Jesus's name, I loose myself from all occult involvement, all sorcery, divination, witchcraft, psychic inheritance, rebellion, all confusion, sickness,*

death, and destruction as a result of occult involvement. Amen.

LOOSE YOUR MIND

For as he thinks in his heart, so is he.
—PROVERBS 23:7

You are the way you think. The mind has always been a favorite target of the enemy. If the devil can control your mind, he can control your life. Spirits that attack the mind include mind control, confusion, mental breakdown, mind-binding and mind-binding spirits, insanity, madness, mania, fantasy, evil thinking, migraines, mental pain, and negative thinking. They are all what I call "stinking thinking."

The good news is that you can loose yourself (including your mind) from all evil influences that operate through your mind. Mind control is a common spirit that has been identified by the name Octopus. Mind control spirits can resemble an octopus or squid with tentacles that grasp and control the mind. Deliverance from mind control releases a person from mental pressure, mental pain, confusion, and mental torment. Mind control spirits can enter through listening to ungodly music, reading occult books, pornography, false teaching, false religions, drugs, and passivity.

Pray:

> *In Jesus's name, I loose my mind from all spirits of control, confusion, mental bondage, insanity, madness, fantasy, passivity, intellectualism, knowledge block, ignorance, mind binding, lust, and evil thinking. Amen.*

PRAYERS AGAINST JEZEBEL

I loose the hounds of heaven against Jezebel (1 Kings 21:23).

I rebuke and bind the spirits of witchcraft, lust, seduction, intimidation, idolatry, and whoredom connected to Jezebel.

I release the spirit of Jehu against Jezebel and her cohorts (2 Kings 9:30–33).

I rebuke all spirits of false teaching, false prophecy, idolatry, and perversion connected with Jezebel (Rev. 2:20).

I loose tribulation against the kingdom of Jezebel (Rev. 2:22).

I cut off the assignment of Jezebel against the ministers of God (1 Kings 19:2).

I cut off and break the powers of every word released by Jezebel against my life.

I cut off Jezebel's table and reject all food from it (1 Kings 18:19).

I cut off and loose myself from all curses of Jezebel and spirits of Jezebel operating in my bloodline.

I cut off the assignment of Jezebel and her daughters to corrupt the church.

I rebuke and cut off the spirit of Athaliah that attempts to destroy the royal seed (2 Kings 11:1).

I come against the spirit of Herodias and cut off the assignment to kill the prophets (Mark 6:22–24).

I rebuke and cut off the spirit of whoredoms (Hos. 4:12).

I rebuke and cut off Jezebel and her witchcrafts in the name of Jesus (2 Kings 9:22).

I rebuke and cut off the harlot and mistress of witchcrafts and break her power over my life and family (Nah. 3:4).

I overcome Jezebel and receive power over the nations (Rev. 2:26).

PRAYERS TO DISANNUL UNGODLY COVENANTS

I break and disannul all ungodly covenants, oaths, and pledges I have made with my lips in the name of Jesus.

I renounce and break all ungodly oaths made by my ancestors to idols, demons, false religions, or ungodly organizations in the name of Jesus (Matt. 5:33).

I break and disannul all covenants with death and hell made by my ancestors in the name of Jesus.

I break and disannul all ungodly covenants made with idols or demons by my ancestors in the name of Jesus (Exod. 23:32).

I break and disannul all blood covenants made through sacrifice that would affect my life in the name of Jesus.

I command all demons that claim any legal right to my life through covenants to come out in the name of Jesus.

I break and disannul any covenant made with false gods and demons through the occult involvement and witchcraft in the name of Jesus.

I break and disannul all spirit marriages that would cause incubus and succubus demons to attack my life in the name of Jesus.

I have a covenant with God through the blood of Jesus Christ. I am joined to the Lord, and I am one spirit with Him. I break all ungodly covenants and renew my covenant to God through the body and blood of Jesus.

Chapter 21

FASTING TO BREAK THE POWER OF A RELIGIOUS SPIRIT

The scribes and the Pharisees sit in Moses' seat. Therefore, whatever they tell you to observe, that observe and do, but do not do their works. For they speak, but do nothing. They fasten heavy loads that are hard to carry and lay them on men's shoulders, but they themselves will not move them with their finger.

—MATTHEW 23:2–4

ONE OF THE most stubborn demons I have seen is a religious spirit—a spirit that causes people to reject change and growth. It causes them to stubbornly hold on to teachings that are not of God. It's hard to teach people who have been taught a certain way all their lives. The religious spirit causes people to be some of the most stubborn people you'll ever meet. One of the things a religious spirit needs to be faced with is that as we grow in God, our revelation of God grows. All of us have to change. We cannot stubbornly hold on to teaching that is contrary to Scripture. We must be humble enough to admit that we don't know everything. All of us are growing and learning. All of us have to change.

There are a lot of things I could talk about that I have had to change in my life in the last years of ministry. And there are things I had to come to grips with that I even preached, that sounded good but weren't really accurate—and I had to change them, because God gave me further light and understanding.

Religious spirits can be so stubborn, but they can be broken through fasting and prayer. The hard part is being able to recognize this spirit in your own life. People bound by a religious spirit have a tendency to judge others and not soberly judge their own sinful condition. If the Lord has given you grace to see past your own blindness to see that you are suffering with this spirit, begin to fast and pray to free yourself once and for all.

PRAYERS THAT BREAK THE POWER OF A RELIGIOUS SPIRIT

I bind and cast out all spirits of judgment, pride, and unteachableness in the name of Jesus.

I bind and cast out all spirits of control and possessiveness in the name of Jesus.

I will not think of myself more highly than I ought to think. But I will remain sober minded (Rom. 12:3).

I remove the religious spirits from the high places (2 Kings 23:8).

I destroy every yoke and burden of religion and legalism placed on my life by religious leaders in the name of Jesus (Matt. 23:4).

I command all religious spirits of doubt, unbelief, error, heresy, and tradition that came in through religion to come out in the name of Jesus.

I bind and cast out all spirits of self-will, selfishness, and stubbornness in the name of Jesus.

I bind and cast out the spirit of accusation in the name of Jesus.

I command all spirits of pride, stubbornness, disobedience, rebellion, self-will, selfishness, and arrogance to come out of my will in the name of Jesus.

I bind and cast out all mind-control spirits of the octopus and squid in the name of Jesus.

Prayers and Declarations
of the Humble

Lord, I am humble. Guide me in justice and teach me Your ways (Ps. 25:9).

I will humble myself in the sight of the Lord, and He will lift me up (James 4:10).

I will not allow pride to enter my heart and cause me shame. I will be humble and clothed in wisdom (Prov. 11:2).

Lord, You take pleasure in me. You beautify me with salvation because I am humble (Ps. 149:4).

Lord, You will look on everyone who is proud, and You will humble them (Job 40:11).

Lord, You will save me (Ps. 18:27).

I will retain honor (Prov. 29:23).

I am better off being of a humble spirit with the lowly than dividing the spoil with the proud (Prov. 16:19).

I will humble myself under the mighty hand of God that He may exalt me in due time (1 Pet. 5:6).

My soul will make its boast in the Lord. The humble will hear of it and be glad (Ps. 34:2).

I will see what God has done and be glad. Because I seek God, my heart will live (Ps. 69:32).

I will not be like Amon, but I will humble myself before the Lord and will not trespass more and more (2 Chron. 33:23).

God, You give more grace. You resist the proud but give grace to the humble (James 4:6).

Let me be like Moses, who was very humble, more than all the men who were on the face of the earth (Num. 12:3).

I will not set my mind on high things, but I will associate with the humble. I will not be wise in my own opinion (Rom. 12:16).

By humility and the fear of the Lord are riches, honor, and life (Prov. 22:4).

I will speak evil of no one. I will be peaceable and gentle, showing all humility to all men (Titus 3:2).

The fear of the Lord is the instruction of wisdom, and before honor is humility (Prov. 15:33).

Before destruction the heart of a man is haughty, and before honor is humility (Prov. 18:12).

As the elect of God, holy and beloved, I will put on tender mercies, kindness, humility, meekness, and longsuffering (Col. 3:12).

I will seek the Lord. I will seek righteousness and humility so that I may be hidden in the day of the Lord's anger (Zeph. 2:3).

I take on the yoke of Christ, learning from Him, for He is meek and lowly in heart (Matt. 11:29).

I will do what the Lord requires of me: I will do justly, love mercy, and walk humbly with my God (Mic. 6:8).

I desire to be like Christ, who humbled Himself and became obedient to the point of death, even the death of the cross (Phil. 2:8).

Chapter 22

FASTING TO BREAK THE SPIRIT OF CARNALITY AND DOUBLE-MINDEDNESS

You adulterers and adulteresses, do you not know that the friendship with the world is enmity with God? Whoever therefore will be a friend of the world is the enemy of God.

—JAMES 4:4

DOUBLE-MINDEDNESS BREEDS WORLDLINESS and carnality. The rejection spirit weds a person to the world for love. It is simply Satan's substitute for true love. Worldliness can be seen in teenage rebellion. Teenagers will often get involved in a lifestyle of lust, perversion, drugs, etc. Parents are often at their wit's end. Signs of double-mindedness can be seen in piercings, tattoos, punk dressing, Goth dressing, provocative clothing, drug addiction, smoking, running away, fighting, gang activity, profanity, disrespect to authority, alternate lifestyles, depression, suicidal tendencies, and withdrawal.

> For a generation now, disruptive young Americans who rebel against authority figures have been increasingly diagnosed with mental illnesses and medicated with psychiatric (psychotropic) drugs.
>
> Disruptive young people who are medicated with Ritalin, Adderall, and other amphetamines routinely report that these drugs make them "care less" about their boredom, resentments and other negative emotions, thus making them more compliant and manageable. And so-called atypical antipsychotics such as Risperdal and Zyprexa—powerful

tranquilizing drugs—are increasingly prescribed to disruptive young Americans, even though in most cases they are not displaying any psychotic symptoms.[1]

Teenage double-mindedness has become an epidemic. Most don't know what they are dealing with. Gods' solution is deliverance and healing. Double-mindedness has also been called passive-aggressive, but it is simply rejection/rebellion.

FASTING BREAKS THE POWERS OF CARNALITY, DIVISION, AND STRIFE

Whose end is destruction, whose god is their belly, and whose glory is in their shame, who mind earthly things.
—PHILIPPIANS 3:19

Carnality is a problem in many families in the body of Christ. To be carnal means to be fleshly. It means to mind earthly things. Carnality refers back to being ruled by our fleshly appetites as I discussed in chapter 16. We should not be controlled by the belly. Fasting takes the power away from the belly and strengthens the spirit. To be carnally minded is death. To be spiritually minded is life and peace (Rom. 8:6). Carnality causes division and strife (1 Cor. 3:13). Carnality hinders believers from growing and coming into maturity. Carnality prevents believers from understanding the deeper truths of the Scriptures.

Fasting helps believers focus on spiritual things. Fasting breaks us free from the power of the flesh. Fasting increases spiritual discernment (1 Cor. 2:15).

BREAKING THE POWER OF
DOUBLE-MINDEDNESS

I bind and rebuke every spirit that would attempt to distort, disturb, or disintegrate the development of my personality in the name of Jesus.

I break all curses of schizophrenia and double-mindedness on my family in the name of Jesus.

I bind and rebuke the spirit of double-mindedness in the name of Jesus (James 1:8).

I bind and take authority over the strongmen of rejection and rebellion and separate them in the name of Jesus.

I bind and cast out the spirits of rejection, fear of rejection, and self-rejection in the name of Jesus.

I bind and cast out all spirits of lust, fantasy lust, harlotry, and perverseness in the name of Jesus.

I bind and cast out all spirits of insecurity and inferiority in the name of Jesus.

I bind and cast out all spirits of self-accusation and compulsive confession in the name of Jesus.

I bind and cast out all spirits of fear of judgment, self-pity, false compassion, and false responsibility in the name of Jesus.

I bind and cast out all spirits of depression, despondency, despair, discouragement, and hopelessness in the name of Jesus.

I bind and cast out all spirits of guilt, condemnation, unworthiness, and shame in the name of Jesus.

I bind and cast out all spirits of perfection, pride, vanity, ego, intolerance, frustration, and impatience in the name of Jesus.

I bind and cast out all spirits of unfairness, withdrawal, pouting, unreality, fantasy, daydreaming, and vivid imagination in the name of Jesus.

I bind and cast out all spirits of self-awareness, timidity, loneliness, and sensitivity in the name of Jesus.

I bind and cast out all spirits of talkativeness, nervousness, tension, and fear in the name of Jesus.

I bind and cast out all spirits of self-will, selfishness, and stubbornness in the name of Jesus.

I bind and cast out the spirit of accusation in the name of Jesus.

I bind and cast out all spirits of self-delusion, self-deception, and self-seduction in the name of Jesus.

I bind and cast out all spirits of judgment, pride, and unteachableness in the name of Jesus.

I bind and cast out all spirits of control and possessiveness in the name of Jesus.

I bind and cast out the root of bitterness in the name of Jesus.

I bind and cast out all spirits of hatred, resentment, violence, murder, unforgiveness, anger, and retaliation in the name of Jesus.

I bind and cast out spirits of paranoia, suspicion, distrust, persecution, confrontation, and fear in the name of Jesus.

Chapter 23

FASTING TO BREAK THE SPIRIT OF PRIDE

But as for me, when they were sick, my clothing was sackcloth; I humbled
my soul with fasting; *and my prayer returned into mine own bosom.*

—Psalm 35:13, emphasis added

ONE OF THE greatest benefits of fasting is the humbling
of the soul. Fasting is a powerful way to humble yourself. Humility is a key to promotion and blessing. James 4:10
says, "Humble yourselves in the sight of the Lord, and he shall
lift you up."

Fasting helps break the power of pride and rebellion. Pride
and rebellion are rampant in our society. Fasting is almost a
lost art. Humility and meekness are seldom seen in the lives
of people.

> Before destruction the heart of man is haughty, and before
> honor is humility.
> —Proverbs 18:12

> Likewise, ye younger, submit yourselves unto the elder.
> Yea, all of you be subject one to another, and be clothed
> with humility: for God resisteth the proud, and giveth
> grace to the humble.
> —1 Peter 5:5, kjv

Humility puts you in a position to receive God's grace.
God's grace is His strength, His power, and His ability.
Fasting will cause God's grace to increase in your life.

PRIDE, SICKNESS, AND
GENERATIONAL SPIRITS

...that He might turn aside man from his purpose, and conceal pride from man. He keeps back his soul from the pit, and his life from perishing by the sword. He is also chastened with pain on his bed, and with strong pain in many of his bones, so that his life abhors bread, and his soul dainty food.

—JOB 33:17–20

Sickness can be a result of pride. Pain can also be a result of pride. Sickness often results in the loss of appetite. This is a forced fast. Fasting humbles the soul. Fasting helps us overcome the strongman of pride. Pride and rebellion are generational spirits that are often difficult to overcome. Gluttony and drunkenness are signs of rebellion (Deut. 21:20).

Rebellion is as the sin of witchcraft (1 Sam. 15:23). God humbled Israel in the wilderness by feeding them with only manna (Deut. 8:3). Israel lusted for meat in the wilderness. This was a manifestation of rebellion (Ps. 106:14–15).

PRAYERS THAT BREAK A PRIDEFUL SPIRIT

May the Lord ruin the pride of Judah and the great pride of Jerusalem (Jer. 13:9).

I break the pride of Moab. It shall no longer be proud of its haughtiness, pride, and wrath. The lies it speaks will not be so (Isa. 16:6).

Thank You, Lord, that You turn me from my deeds and conceal my pride from me so that my soul may be kept back from the pit and my life from perishing by the sword (Job 33:17).

Lord, I break the spirit of pride. Please answer when I cry out (Job 35:12).

I rebuke the shame that comes from a spirit of pride (Prov. 11:2).

I come against strife that comes with the spirit of pride (Prov. 13:10).

I break the spirit of pride, so that I will not fall and be destroyed (Prov. 16:18).

I break the spirit of pride. It will not bring me low. I will have a humble spirit (Prov. 29:23).

Pride will not serve as my necklace, nor will violence cover me like a garment (Ps. 73:6).

I will not be puffed up with pride and fall into the same condemnation as the devil (1 Tim. 3:6).

I break pride off of my life in the name of Jesus. I will not stumble in my iniquity like Israel, Ephraim, and Judah (Hosea 5:5).

The spirit of pride will not rule me. I shall not be desolate in the day of rebuke (Hosea 5:9).

The spirit of pride will not cause me to be scattered (Luke 1:51).

The Lord is above the spirit of the proud (Exod. 18:11).

Hear and give ear, spirit of pride. The Lord has spoken (Jer. 13:15).

I command the spirit of pride to cease its persecution of the poor. Let that spirit be caught in the plots it has devised (Ps. 10:2).

Let not the foot of pride come against me, and let not the hand of the wicked drive me away (Ps. 36:11).

The Lord will break the power of pride; He will make my heavens like iron and my earth like bronze (Lev. 26:19).

Let the pride of Israel be broken in the name of Jesus.

Let them not testify to His face then go on not returning to the Lord their God (Hosea 7:10).

Lord, bring dishonor to the spirit of pride and bring into contempt all the honorable of the earth (Isa. 23:9).

I fear the Lord; therefore, I hate evil, pride, arrogance, and the evil way. I hate the perverse mouth (Prov. 8:13).

I break the spirit of the pride of life, for it is not of the Father but is of the world (1 John 2:16).

I will not be wise in my own eyes (Prov. 26:12).

Let the crown of pride, the drunkards of Ephraim, be trampled under foot (Isa. 28:3).

Like a swimmer reaches out to swim, Lord, spread out Your hands in their midst and bring down the prideful and their trickery (Isa. 25:11).

Like King Hezekiah, let prideful leaders humble themselves so that the wrath of the Lord does not come upon the people (2 Chron. 32:26).

Let not the pride of my heart deceive me. I have been brought low to the ground (Obad. 3).

The proud in heart are an abomination to the Lord. Let them not go unpunished (Prov. 16:5).

Let all their cities and everything in them be given to their enemies (Amos 6:8).

Those who walk in pride will be put down by the King of heaven (Dan. 4:37).

Those who uphold Egypt will fall; the pride of her power will come down, and those within her shall fall by the sword (Ezek. 30:6).

I come against the spirit of the proud and haughty man who acts with arrogant pride (Prov. 21:24).

The Lord will bring down haughty looks (Ps. 18:27).

Let the most proud stumble and fall, and no one raise him up. Let the Lord kindle a fire in his cities, and it will devour all around him (Jer. 50:32).

I will let another man praise me, and not my own mouth; a stranger, and not my own lips (Prov. 27:2).

I dare not class myself or compare myself with those who commend themselves. They are not wise (2 Cor. 10:12).

I do not respect the proud or those who turn aside to lies. I make the Lord my trust (Ps. 40:4).

Lord, my heart is not haughty (Ps. 131:1).

Let the Lord halt the arrogance of the proud and lay low the haughtiness of the terrible (Isa. 13:11).

The Lord will not endure a haughty look and a proud heart (Ps. 101:5).

I will not talk proudly and will let no arrogance come from my mouth (1 Sam. 2:3).

The Lord resists the proud. Let me be like the humble one who receives grace from God (James 4:6).

Chapter 24

FASTING TO BREAK CHRONIC CYCLES OF BACKSLIDING

*Now the just shall live by faith; but if anyone draws
back, my soul shall have no pleasure in him.*

—HEBREWS 10:38

BACKSLIDING AND AN inconsistent walk of faith are signs of double-mindedness, wavering between two lifestyles. I have seen this as a pattern for many believers. I have seen believers commit to Christ and then turn away and return to the world. They then return and repeat the process over again. This is heartbreaking.

This was also an issue for the early church. Many believers were departing from the faith and returning to the old covenant system. They were wavering in their faith. These Christians were also fighting and warring with one another, and James commanded them to humble themselves and cleanse their hands (James 4). Notice in this same passage that the spirits of lust and pride are prevalent in the double-minded, and there is contention, strife, and adultery. Adultery is unfaithfulness to covenant and can refer to backsliding and apostasy. Some of these believers were leaving Christ and returning to the world; James referred to them as sinners (v. 8).

Double-mindedness breeds unbelief and doubt. Backsliding and apostasy can be signs of double-mindedness. The prophet Jeremiah revealed that the remedy to backsliding is healing—in other words, deliverance (Jer. 3:22).

Are you double-minded in your walk with Christ? Do you have a history of backsliding and departing from the faith? Are you guilty of worldliness and carnality? Do you crack under pressure or persecution and return to the things of the world? These are all signs of double-mindedness.

The double-minded are not stable enough to deal with the challenges that often come with being a believer. They will often withdraw or rebel. We must become stable if we are to walk with God consistently. Deliverance is the answer, and I am committed to seeing this truth taught in the church.

A closer look at backsliding in the Old and New Testaments

The Hebrew words for the term backsliding are *mshuwbah*, meaning "apostasy: backsliding, turning away,"[1] and *sarar*, meaning "to turn away, i.e. (morally) be refractory—X away, backsliding, rebellious, revolter(-ing), slide back, stubborn, withdrew."[2] Other words from the Hebrew, *shobab* and *shobeb*, render the English meanings "apostate, i.e. idolatrous—backsliding, frowardly, turn away (from margin);" "heathenish or (actually) heathen—backsliding."[3]

Israel was a double-minded nation, going in and out of covenant with God. They were not consistent in their loyalty to God. Israel was guilty of revolt, rebellion, turning away, stubbornness, idolatry, and acting like the heathen nations that surrounded it. This leaves me no doubt that chronic backsliding is a manifestation of double-mindedness.

Fasting Can Restore Your Covenant With God

> Now in the twenty-fourth day of this month the children of Israel were assembled with fasting, in sackcloth, and with dust upon their head.... "And because of all this, we make a sure covenant and write it; our leaders, our Levites, and our priests, seal it."
>
> —Nehemiah 9:1, 38

Fasting is a way we can renew covenant with the Lord. Fasting helps fallen believers become restored. Fasting is a part of renewing our commitment to the things of God.

Prayers of Repentance

Lord, I repent in dust and ashes (Job 42:6).

I will repent so that I won't perish (Luke 13:3).

I repent for my wickedness and pray that the thoughts of my heart be forgiven me (Acts 8:22).

I will not tolerate the spirit of Jezebel in my life. I will not suffer anguish because of her adultery. I will repent and hold fast to what I have (Rev. 2:20–25).

Thank You, Lord, that my sins have been blotted out and times of refreshing have come from Your presence, because I have repented and been converted (Acts 3:19).

Lord, I repent. Do not remove my lampstand from its place (Rev. 2:5).

I receive the gift of the Holy Spirit, because I have repented and have been baptized (Acts 2:38).

Lord, I repent, for Your kingdom is at hand (Matt. 3:2).

Lord, I repent, that Your mighty works will be done in me (Matt. 11:20).

I will be zealous and repent because You love me and chasten me (Rev. 3:19).

I will turn to God and do the works befitting repentance (Acts 26:20).

I repent now for You will not always overlook my ignorance (Acts 17:30).

The Assyrian will not be my king, because I willingly repent (Hosea 11:5).

I repent and believe in the gospel (Mark 1:1).

I repent now of my evil way and evil doings that I may dwell in the land that the Lord has given to me and my fathers forever (Jer. 25:5).

I repent, Lord, and turn away from my idols and all my abominations (Ezek. 14:6).

Do not judge me, O Lord. I repent and turn from all my transgressions so that iniquity will not be my ruin (Ezek. 18:30).

I repent and make supplication to You, Lord, saying, "I have sinned and done wrong. I have committed wickedness" (1 Kings 8:47).

I remember what I have received and heard. I hold fast, repent, and remain watchful (Rev. 3:3).

Let repentance and remission of sins be preached in His name to all nations (Luke 24:47).

I repent before God and remain faithful toward my Lord Jesus Christ (Acts 20:21).

Godly sorrow produces repentance leading to salvation. I will not regret it (2 Cor. 7:10).

The Lord gives repentance to Israel and forgiveness of sins (Acts 5:31).

I will arise and go to my Father, and I will say to Him, "Father, I have sinned against heaven and before You" (Luke 15:18).

PRAYERS TO ACTIVATE GOD'S COVENANT IN YOUR LIFE

Shalom, prosperity, and peace are mine through Jesus Christ.

I am a saint of God.

I am a child of God.

I have a covenant with God.

My covenant is a covenant of peace, prosperity, and blessing.

I walk in covenant all the days of my life.

I enjoy shalom, prosperity, peace, and safety all the days of my life.

I will walk in covenant.

I will be faithful to the covenant through the blood of Jesus.

I have a covenant of shalom, peace, and prosperity, in my life.

Lord, You keep covenant and mercy with those who love You and keep Your commandments (Exod. 20).

Lord, You bless those who obey Your voice and keep Your covenant.

Lord, I take hold of Your covenant through Your death and sacrifice.

I choose life (blessing) (Deut. 30:19).

Let Your blessings come upon me and overtake me (Deut. 28:2).

Let me be blessed in the city and blessed in the field (Deut. 28:3).

Let the fruit of my body be blessed, and let all the fruit of my labor be blessed (Deut. 28:4).

Let my basket and store be blessed (Deut. 28:5, KJV).

Let me be blessed coming in and blessed going out (Deut. 28:6).

Let the enemies of my soul flee before me seven ways (Deut. 28:7).

Command Your blessing upon my storehouses and all I set my hand to, and bless my land (Deut. 28:8).

Establish me as a holy person unto You, Lord (Deut. 28:9).

Let all people see that I am called by Your name (Deut. 28:10).

Make me plenteous in goods (Deut. 28:11).

Open unto me Your good treasure, and let heaven's rain fall upon my life and bless the work of my hand (Deut. 28:12).

Let me lend (give) unto many nations and not borrow (Deut. 28:12).

Make me the head and not the tail (Deut. 28:13).

Let me be above only and not beneath (Deut. 28:13).

Chapter 25

FASTING FOR BREAKTHROUGH IN MARRIAGE

What therefore God has joined together, let not man put asunder.

—MARK 10:9

DOUBLE-MINDEDNESS AFFECTS OUR ability to honor and stay true to covenant. Covenant requires stability, loyalty, and faithfulness. How can we walk in covenant if we are double-minded? How can we have strong covenant relationships if we are double-minded? God is a covenant-keeping God, and our relationship with Him is based on covenant.

Marriage is a covenant between a husband and a wife. Is it any wonder that we have so many divorces in and out of the church? There are too many unstable people entering into marriages. Double-minded people will have instability in their marriages. We will continue to see troubled marriages unless double-mindedness is dealt with. With a large number of marriages ending in divorce, it is no surprise that double-mindedness is a major problem.

> They sharpen their tongue like a sword, and bend their bows to shoot their arrows—bitter words, that they may shoot in secret at the blameless; suddenly they shoot at him and do not fear.
>
> —PSALM 64:3–4

People who are bitter speak cruel things that will hurt you. A bitter husband uses his tongue to cut up his wife. A bitter wife will do the same thing. The words of a bitter person become like arrows that pierce the hearts of others around them. That's why it is so terrible to have bitterness in a marriage. A couple who is bitter at each other will speak words to one another that are so sharp and cruel until wounds of hurt and broken-heartedness are opened up. Words hurt.

The Bible says, "Husbands love your wives" (Eph. 5:25). Love is kind. Love speaks kind words. Then in Colossians 3:19, husbands are directed to not only love them but also warned, "Do not be bitter toward them." The Spirit of God specifically tells husbands not to be bitter toward their wives because there is a tendency and a temptation for men who are married, if they are bitter, to take it out on their wives. Bitter men are the cause of many marital problems and divorces.

This doesn't mean that women can't be bitter. Anyone can have the spirit of bitterness, but this particular scripture specifically tells men not to be bitter toward their wives. Having dealt with many women in counseling, I've talked with women who are wondering why their husbands are so abusive—verbally, physically—and treat them in a cruel way. Often the root cause of that man's mistreatment of his wife is that he has not dealt with that bitterness in his own life.

When you are bitter you become angry and abusive. Because a husband and wife are close—marriage is the closest covenant you can have—it is often that women suffer because men have not dealt with their bitterness. A man's bitterness destroys his marriage and his family. It has an effect on his children. While bitterness does oppress both men and women, I tend to focus more on men because in life you run across many men who have not dealt with it.

A word to husbands and fathers

There are a lot of double-minded men who are married and have children. Families need strong, steadfast men. Men are called to be the providers and protectors of the family. When trouble comes, the husband and father should be able to stand up and say, "Honey, I got this. Don't worry, baby. Children, don't worry. It's all right. I believe God. I pray. I bind. I loose. I take authority over the devil. I'm the head of my house. Devil, you cannot have my wife, my kids, or my family. You will not destroy us, because I trust in God. I am the covering. I am the head of this house."

Yet what we too frequently find is weak, double-minded men who let their wives go to church and do all the praying and believing, while they stay home watching football. Then when spiritual trouble comes, they don't know how to pray, bind the devil, loose, stand up for anything, recite a scripture, or anything else. They leave their families vulnerable to attack.

Kingdom families need godly men who will stand up and say, "I fear the Lord. My heart is fixed. I will not be moved. I'm a godly man. I'm not double-minded. I am single-minded. I've already made the decision. I am established in God. I am not wavering. I am not doubting. I believe God. I take the shield of faith, and I quench every fiery dart of the wicked one. I am not an Ahab, double-minded man."

I especially challenge men to take hold of the message in this book. I challenge men to stand up and be single-minded. Get healed and delivered from double-mindedness and allow God to stabilize you so that your personality becomes matured in Christ. Like the Psalm 112 believer, you can be the man who does not fear evil tidings, because your heart is fixed, trusting in the Lord. Set your heart upon God. Make the clear decision to serve God and love Him with all your heart. Be a man of God. Love His Word. Love His Spirit. Love what is right and holy. Love the things of God. Declare that you will not be ashamed to be a man of God in all your ways, never compromising.

Other men may waver and be drunkards, whoremongers, liars, and cheaters. Other men may not want to get married, raise their children, or keep covenant. But that is not who you have to be, man of God. That is not what you should want to do. You can be a man of God, who loves his wife, loves his children, loves people, is holy and clean, loves to pray, loves to worship, loves to sing, and loves to talk about the things of God. Yes, you can be a man of God, whose heart is fixed. You can know who you are. You can be sure of what you believe and in whom you have believed. You can be stable.

PRAYERS FOR A STRONG MARRIAGE

I break and release myself from all curses of divorce and separation.

I take authority over my thoughts and bind all spirits of fantasy and lustful thinking in the name of Jesus.

I cast out all marriage-breaking spirits of lust that would break covenant in the name of Jesus.

Father, the spirit of Jezebel is a seducing spirit that is causing rampant destruction in America today. Teach me to "honor marriage, and guard the sacredness of sexual intimacy between wife and husband." May I never forget that "God draws a firm line against casual and illicit sex" (Heb. 13:4, THE MESSAGE).

Father, Your Word teaches the painful lesson of the evil influence of Jezebel. Although King Jehoshaphat loved and served You throughout his life, his son Jehoram, who became king after him, married the daughter of wicked Queen Jezebel. Jehoram was influenced by this evil generational spirit and led his kingdom into worshipping false gods and falling into gross immorality in their lives (2 Chron. 21:11). As a result, You caused him to die of a painful stomach disease. Lord, help us to lead our children into godly marriages and to teach them the consequences of becoming unequally yoked in marriage with the evil spirit of Jezebel at work in a person's life.

Father, You teach in Your Word, "'Whoever divorces his wife, let him give her a certificate of divorce.' But I say to you that whoever divorces his wife for any reason except sexual immorality causes her to commit adultery; and whoever marries a woman who is divorced commits adultery" (Matt. 5:31–32, NKJV). Stop the evil influence of Belial at work in America causing men and women to engage in adulterous relationships and sexual immorality. Belial seeks the destruction of Your divine institution of marriage. Keep me pure in my relationships, and let me join the fight to save marriage in America.

Father, You wrote to the church at Thyatira, "I know everything about you, including your love, your faith, your service, and how you have endured. I know that you are doing more now than you have ever done before. But I still have something against you because of that woman Jezebel. She calls herself a prophet, and you let her teach and mislead my servants to do immoral things and to eat food offered to idols. I gave her a chance to turn from her sins, but she did not want to stop doing these immoral things. I am going to strike down Jezebel. Everyone who does these immoral things with her will also be punished, if they don't stop" (Rev. 2:19–22, CEV). Examine my heart, Lord, and show me my heart. If the spirit of Jezebel is present in my life, I repent, and I plead for Your forgiveness. And if that evil spirit has somehow crept into my family and influenced my family members with her evil teachings, reveal that to me, and cast it out of my home. I want my love for You and my family's love for You to be pure and holy in Your sight.

Chapter 26

FASTING TO RESTORE
WHAT'S BEEN LOST

So we fasted and sought our God for this, and He was moved by our prayers.

—Ezra 8:23

Ezra and Nehemiah were instrumental in the restoration of the city of Jerusalem after captivity. They prayed and fasted to see breakthrough. Fasting is a key to restoration. *Restore* means to bring back to health. Synonyms include *freshen, recharge, recreate, refresh, refreshen, regenerate.*

Broken walls represent broken lives. People who have experienced broken walls in their lives can be restored with the help of fasting. Fasting helps in healing and restoration.

> And they that shall be of thee shall build the old waste places: thou shalt raise up the foundations of many generations; and thou shalt be called, the repairer of the breach, the restorer of paths to dwell in.
>
> —Isaiah 58:12, kjv

> And I will restore to you the years that the locust hath eaten, the cankerworm, and the caterpillar, and the palmerworm, my great army which I sent among you.
>
> —Joel 2:25, kjv

Fasting can help restore your joy, your strength, your victory, your power, your health, and your anointing. If you have lost your joy, your zeal, your passion, your victory, then I encourage fasting.

Fasting Closes Breaches and Brings Forth Restoration and Rebuilding

Those from among you shall rebuild the old waste places; you shall raise up the foundations of many generations; and you shall be called, the Repairer of the Breach, the Restorer of Paths in which to Dwell.

—Isaiah 58:12

When I heard these words, I sat down and wept and mourned for days. Then I fasted, and prayed before the God of heaven.

—Nehemiah 1:4

There are many believers who need restoration. They need restoration in their families, finances, relationships, health, and walk with the Lord. Fasting is a part of restoration. Fasting closes the breaches. Breaches are gaps in the wall that give the enemy an entry point into our lives. Breaches need to be repaired and closed. When the breaches are closed, the enemy no longer has an opening to attack.

Fasting also helps keep us on the right path (Isa. 58:12). Fasting helps to prevent us from going astray. Fasting will help those who have strayed from the right path to return. Fasting is a cure for backsliding.

Fasting helps us to walk in the good path (Prov. 2:9), the path of life (v. 19), the path of peace (Prov. 3:17), the old path (Jer. 6:16), and the straight path (Heb. 12:13). Fasting restores these paths and helps us to walk in them.

In Nehemiah 1 we see that Nehemiah's journey to restore and rebuild the walls in Jerusalem began with fasting. Fasting initiated the events that made his plans possible. Fasting will be an asset to anyone with a desire to see restoration in the lives of people who have experienced desolation.

Fasting helps restore and rebuild the walls in our lives that have been broken down. Walls are symbolic of protection and safety. A city without walls is open for attack from the enemy (Prov. 25:28). Fasting helps restore the walls of salvation (Isa. 60:18). Fasting helps restore watchmen to the walls (Isa. 62:6).

PRAYERS THAT CLOSE
BREACHES AND HEDGES

I close up any breach in my life that would give Satan and demons access in the name of Jesus (Eccles. 10:8).

I pray for every broken hedge in my life to be restored in the name of Jesus (Eccles. 10:8).

I stand in the gap and make up the hedge (Ezek. 22:30).

I repent and receive forgiveness for any sin that has opened the door for any spirit to enter and operate in my life (Eph. 4:27).

I am a rebuilder of the wall and a repairer of the breach (Isa. 58:12).

I renounce all crooked speech that would cause a breach in the name of Jesus (Prov. 15:4).

Bind up all my breaches, O Lord (Isa. 30:26).

Let every breach be stopped in the name of Jesus (Neh. 4:7).

Let my walls be salvation and my gates praise (Isa. 60:18).

I pray for a hedge of protection around my mind, body, finances, possessions, and family in the name of Jesus.

Chapter 27

FASTING FOR BREAKTHROUGH IN THE LIVES OF YOUR CHILDREN

And all thy children shall be taught of the LORD; and
great shall be the peace of thy children.

—ISAIAH 54:13, KJV

T HE SPIRITUAL AND personal success of our children is the focus of many of the prayers believers pray. We hope for the best. Yet there are times when they need the strength of our faith in God's promises over their lives. There are times when what they face requires us to activate our spiritual wisdom and maturity on their behalf. We can stand in the gap for our children by fasting and praying for their salvation, deliverance, safety, healing, success, and breakthrough. Angels will be dispatched to intervene in their lives and deliver to them the future and hope God promised.

Do not lose hope if your children are far from the Lord. Your prayer and fasting can bring about the full measure of salvation in their lives. Your fasting can deactivate and reverse the weapons the enemy tries to form against them. They will be taught by the Lord. They will not depart from the way of the Lord. Fasting restores breaches and gaps. Fasting brings deliverance and salvation to households. Fasting is a cure for backsliding. The Lord is faithful to His covenant with you. He keeps His promises.

As you fast and pray on behalf of your children, ask the Lord to give you spiritual eyes through which to see your children. Do not let what you see in the natural shake your faith for what you know the Lord has promised.

FASTING WILL RELEASE GOD'S GLORY FOR YOUR AND YOUR CHILDREN'S PROTECTION

> Then your salvation will come like the dawn, and your wounds will quickly heal. Your godliness will lead you forward, and the glory of the LORD will protect you from behind.
>
> —ISAIAH 58:8, NLT

Throughout this book, I have used verses from Isaiah 58 as a foundation because it is the Lord giving instruction on what is His chosen fast. There are many promises revealed here that God will honor and keep when we fast. Divine protection is another promise from Isaiah 58.

God promises to protect us with His glory. Fasting releases the glory of the Lord, which covers us. God has promised to cover the church with glory as a defense (Isa. 4:5). The enemy cannot penetrate or overcome this glory.

Fasting will prepare the way for you and your children and deliver you from enemies that lie in wait.

> Then I proclaimed a fast there, at the river of Ahava, that we might humble ourselves before our God, to seek from Him a good route for us, our little ones, and all our substance.... Then we began the journey from the Ahava River on the twelfth day of the first month to go to Jerusalem. The hand of our God was upon us, and He delivered us from the hand of the attacker and the ambusher along the way.
>
> —EZRA 8:21, 31

The prophet Ezra fasted because he recognized the danger of his mission. Fasting will protect you and your children from the plans of the enemy. Fasting will stop the ambush of the enemy. Fasting will cause your substance to be protected from the attack of the enemy.

Wisdom Confessions to Declare Over Your Children

My children receive the wisdom of God and the fear of the Lord. Let them be a part of their lives.

My children will make wise decisions.

My children will know the Word of God.

I believe that wisdom is my children's companion.

Wisdom will bless them.

Wisdom will protect them.

Wisdom will promote them.

Wisdom will exalt them.

Wisdom is the principal thing.

My children receive wisdom, the wisdom of the Word, the Spirit of wisdom.

Jesus is their wisdom.

He's in their life.

My children receive the wisdom of heaven to walk on the earth.

Thank You, Lord, for blessing my children with wisdom.

My children will not make foolish decisions.

My children will not make foolish choices.

My children will not have foolish relationships.

My children walk in wisdom all the days of their lives, and they are blessed in Jesus's name.

Lord, teach my children wisdom's ways and lead them in straight paths (Prov. 4:11).

The Lord's wisdom will save my children's lives (Eccles. 7:12).

My children will have an understanding heart that is enshrined in wisdom (Prov. 14:33).

My children tune their ears to Your wisdom, Lord, and concentrate on understanding (Prov. 2:2, NLT).

My children do not put their trust in human wisdom but in the power of God (1 Cor. 2:5).

In You, O Lord, lie the hidden treasures of wisdom and knowledge (Col. 2:3).

My children listen when those who are older speak, for wisdom comes with age (Job 32:7).

Lord, Your wisdom is more profitable than silver, and its wages are better than gold (Prov. 3:14).

Let wisdom multiply my children's days and add years to their lives (Prov. 9:11).

Let my children's houses be built by wisdom and become strong through good sense (Prov. 24:3).

My children will not be foolish and trust their own insight, but they will walk in wisdom and be safe (Prov. 28:26).

Let the fruit of my children's lives prove Your wisdom is right (Luke 7:35).

Let the fear of the Lord teach my children wisdom (Prov. 15:33).

My children will obey Your commands, so that they will grow in wisdom (Ps. 111:10).

Fill my children with Your Spirit, O God, and give them great wisdom, ability, and expertise in all kinds of crafts (Exod. 31:3).

Lord, give my children wisdom and knowledge to lead effectively (2 Chron. 1:10).

Let those who have gone before my children teach them wisdom of old (Job 8:8–10).

True wisdom and power are found in You, God (Job 12:13).

The price of Your wisdom, O Lord, cannot be purchased with jewels mounted in fine gold; its price is far above rubies (Job 28:17–18).

My children will keep silent, O God. Teach them wisdom (Job 33:33).

Your wisdom will save my children from evil people and from the immoral woman (Prov. 2:12, 16).

My children will embrace Your wisdom, for it is happiness and a tree of life to them (Prov. 3:18).

My children will pay attention to Your wisdom, O Lord. They will listen carefully to Your wise counsel (Prov. 5:1).

Give my children understanding so that Your knowledge and wisdom will come easily to them (Prov. 14:6).

Grant my children wisdom so that they may also have good judgment, knowledge, and discernment (Prov. 8:12).

Thank You, Lord, that You will certainly give my children the wisdom and knowledge they have requested (2 Chron. 1:12).

My children will not be impressed with their own wisdom, but they will fear the Lord and turn away from evil (Prov. 3:7).

My children will not turn their backs on Your wisdom, O God, for it will protect and guard them (Prov. 4:6).

Your wisdom is better than strength (Eccles. 9:16).

I thank and praise You, God of my ancestors, for You have given my children wisdom and strength (Dan. 2:23).

For You will give my children the right words and such wisdom that none of their opponents will be able to reply or refute them (Luke 21:15).

My children need wisdom; therefore, I will ask my generous God, and He will give it to them. He will not rebuke me for asking (James 1:5).

I pray that my children's lives please You, O God, that You might grant them wisdom, knowledge, and joy (Eccles. 2:26).

PRAYERS FOR YOUR CHILDREN TO WALK IN DIVINE FAVOR

Father, I thank You for Your favor. I believe in the power of favor.

I humble myself and ask for Your favor on my children. They need Your favor in every area of their lives.

I believe my children are increasing in favor. I declare that they desire to walk in higher levels of favor. They receive an abundance of favor, and they reign in life through Your favor. They receive great favor.

As my children grow in the knowledge of You and the Lord Jesus Christ, I believe favor is multiplied unto them. They are givers. As they give, Your favor abounds toward them. I declare that they are merciful and trustworthy. They have favor with God and man.

I believe You will support, endorse, help, make things easier, promote, and honor my children because of Your favor. They will enjoy "favored child" status from their heavenly Father. Your favor surrounds my children as a shield.

Your favor overflows in my children's lives. Thank You, Father, for Your favor on them.

I praise You and give You glory for Your favor on my children's lives.

Lord, You have granted my children life and favor.

I thank You for favor coming upon my children's lives.

I believe that new life and new favor have been ordained for my children.

Today my children receive new life and new favor.

I believe favor is a gift of heaven.

My children receive the gift of life—the gift of eternal life.

My children receive the gift of favor and the gift of grace upon their lives in the name of Jesus.

Thank You, Lord, for new grace and new favor, new prosperity and new blessing coming on my children's lives.

My children are the apple of God's eye.

My children are God's favorites.

God favors, loves, and has chosen my children from the foundation of the world to receive His grace and favor.

My children receive extraordinary favor on their lives in the name of Jesus!

Let my children be well favored (Gen. 39:6).

Lord, show my children mercy and give them favor (Gen. 39:21).

Give my children favor in the sight of the world (Exod. 12:36).

Let my children be satisfied with Your favor like Naphtali (Deut. 33:23).

Let my children have favor with You, Lord, and with men (1 Sam. 2:26).

Let my children have favor with the king (1 Sam. 16:22).

Let my children have great favor in the sight of the king (1 Kings 11:19).

Let my children find favor like Esther (Esther 2:17).

Thou hast granted my children life and favour, and Thy visitation hath preserved their spirits (Job 10:12, KJV).

I pray unto You, Lord, grant my children favor (Job 33:26).

Bless my children and surround them with favor like a shield (Ps. 5:12).

In Your favor is life (Ps. 30:5).

Make my children's mountain stand strong by Your favor (Ps. 30:7).

Because of Your favor, the enemy will not triumph over my children (Ps. 41:11).

Through Your favor, my children are brought back from captivity (Ps. 85:1).

Let the horn of my children be exalted through Your favor (Ps. 89:17).

My children's set time of favor has come (Ps. 102:13).

I entreat Your favor on behalf of my children with my whole heart (Ps. 119:58).

Let Your favor be for my children as a cloud of the latter rain (Prov. 16:15).

Let Your favor be upon my children's lives as the dew upon the grass (Prov. 19:12).

My children choose Your loving favor rather than gold and silver (Prov. 22:1).

Let my children be highly favored (Luke 1:28).

Chapter 28

FASTING TO SEE SALVATION COME TO UNSAVED LOVED ONES

While praying also for us, that God would open to us a door of utterance to speak the mystery of Christ, for which I am also in chains.

—COLOSSIANS 4:3

DOORS ARE ENTRY points that provide access. God's access into a family can come through one person. Every person is connected to someone else, and everyone has some influence in another's life. Families consist of strong interpersonal relationships that God uses to connect people to the gospel and salvation.

Throughout the New Testament the words *save*, *saved*, and *salvation* have their root in the Greek *sozo*, which means to save, to rescue, to deliver, to protect. *Sozo* is also translated in the New Testament with the words to heal, preserve, save, do well, and to make whole. The Greek *soteria* (which has its origin in *sozo*) is the main word translated "salvation." *Soteria* is also translated to deliver, health, salvation, save, and saving.

Sozo, which is used one hundred ten times in the New Testament, is originally a Greek word meaning, "to save or make well or whole." According to the Strong's *sozo* also means, "to save, deliver, heal preserve." The writers of the New Testament showed the completeness of the word *sozo* by using it in different contexts to refer to each aspect of salvation.

1. To save, keep safe and sound, to rescue one from danger or destruction (from injury or peril)

145

2. To save a suffering one (from perishing), i.e., one suffering from disease, to make well, heal, restore to health

3. To preserve one who is in danger of destruction, to save or rescue

4. To save in the technical biblical sense

5. To deliver from the penalties of the Messianic judgment

6. To save from the evils that obstruct the reception of the Messianic deliverance

A covenant believer can open the doors of salvation to his or her family by walking with God the way Abraham did. A covenant believer can walk in obedience and faith. A covenant believer can intercede on his family's behalf and expect God to heal and deliver. God hears the prayers of the righteous. He is friends with the faithful. The full measure of salvation is extended to your family because of covenant.

There are numerous examples in Scripture of salvation coming to a household. This has been seen throughout history with God's Word coming to countless households. Only eternity will reveal the number of households that have been saved over generations. The good news is that God desires to visit and save your household as well.

> When you enter a house, first say, "Peace be to this house."
> If a son of peace is there, your peace will rest upon him;
> but if not, it will return upon you.
>
> —Luke 10:5–6

Shalom (peace) can come to a house. The gospel is the gospel of peace. Salvation brings peace. Peace is the word shalom, meaning health, favor, and wholeness. This is God's desire for households that believe the gospel of peace.

PRAYERS FOR FAMILY SALVATION

God, You are the faithful God, the covenant-keeping God. You keep covenant and loyalty to a thousand generations. I have a covenant with You through the blood of Jesus, which provides salvation, forgiveness, and blessing to my life. You promised Abraham that through his seed all families of the earth would be blessed. Jesus is the promised seed, and through Him my family can be blessed.

I come before You on the behalf of my family, and ask for Your salvation, protection, deliverance, and healing to manifest in my family. I pray for anyone in my family who is not in covenant with You to be drawn to You by Your Spirit and to accept Jesus as Lord and Savior. I pray for covenant blessing to come to my family and that my family would benefit from covenant blessings.

Have mercy upon my family, and let Your lovingkindness and tender mercy be over us. Let Your grace and favor be upon my family. Let my family in this generation be blessed, and let generations to come walk in covenant with You and be blessed.

Lord, save my family.

Lord, let Your Word come to every family member, and let them believe.

I bind and rebuke every demon that has been assigned to my family members to prevent them from receiving salvation.

Lord, let salvation come to my household. Let my household be like the household of Obed-Edom (2 Sam. 6:11).

DECLARE THE SALVATION OF THE LORD OVER YOUR FAMILY

My family is waiting for Your salvation, O Lord (Gen. 49:18).

My family hopes for the salvation of the Lord, and we do His commandments (Ps. 119:166).

My eyes have seen the salvation of the Lord for my family (Luke 2:30).

The Lord is the rock and salvation for my family. He is our defense, and we will not be moved (Ps. 62:6).

Salvation belongs to the Lord, and His blessing is upon my family (Ps. 3:8).

My family trusts in the Lord's mercy, and our hearts rejoice in His salvation (Ps. 13:5).

My family rejoices in the Lord's salvation (Ps. 35:9).

The Lord, our salvation, makes haste to help my family (Ps. 38:22).

The Lord will restore to my family the joy of His salvation and will uphold us by His generous Spirit (Ps. 51:12).

Let the way of the Lord be made known in my family and His salvation among us all (Ps. 67:2).

The Lord works salvation in our midst (Ps. 74:12).

The Lord shows mercy to my family and grants us His salvation (Ps. 85:7).

The Lord will satisfy my family with long life, and He will show us His salvation (Ps. 91:16).

My family seeks diligently the salvation of the Lord and His righteous word (Ps. 119:123).

My family praises You, O Lord, for You have answered us and have become our salvation (Ps. 118:21).

My family longs for the salvation of the Lord, and His law is our delight (Ps. 119:174).

My family hopes and waits quietly for the salvation of the Lord (Lam. 3:26).

The Lord has risen up a horn of salvation for my family (Luke 1:69).

By the remission of their sins, the knowledge of salvation is given to my family (Luke 1:77).

The grace of God, which brings salvation, has appeared to my family (Titus 2:11).

Jesus is the author of eternal salvation for my family because we obey Him (Heb. 5:9).

God is my family's salvation. We will trust and not be afraid. The Lord is our strength and song (Isa. 12:2).

The Lord will bring His righteousness near to my family. It will not be far off. His salvation will not linger. He will place salvation in us, for we are His glory (Isa. 46:13).

Truly, the Lord our God is the salvation of my family (Jer. 3:23).

The Lord has given my family the shield of His salvation (2 Sam. 22:36).

The Lord is the rock of salvation for my family (2 Sam. 22:47).

The Lord is the tower of salvation for my family. He shows us and our descendants His mercy (2 Sam. 22:51).

My family will sing to the Lord and proclaim the good news of His salvation from day to day (1 Chron. 16:23).

My family rejoices in the Lord's salvation (Ps. 9:14).

The glory of my family is great in the salvation of the Lord. Honor and majesty have been placed upon us (Ps. 21:5).

My family waits on the Lord all the day, for He is the God of our salvation (Ps. 25:5).

The God of my family's salvation loads us daily with benefits (Ps. 68:19).

The God of our salvation will restore us and cause His anger toward us to cease (Ps. 85:4).

The Lord's salvation is near to my family, because we fear Him. His glory dwells in our land (Ps. 85:9).

The Lord has remembered His mercy and faithfulness to my family. We have seen His salvation (Ps. 98:3).

The Lord will remember my family with His favor and visit us with His salvation (Ps. 106:4).

My family will take up the cup of salvation and will call upon the name of the Lord (Ps. 116:13).

The Lord's salvation will come upon my family according to His word (Ps. 119:41).

The Lord has clothed the priests in my family with salvation (Ps. 132:16).

The Lord is the strength of our salvation. He covers our heads in the day of battle (Ps. 140:7).

The Lord takes pleasure in my family and beautifies us with His salvation (Ps. 149:4).

The Lord's salvation is about to come to my family, and His righteousness will be revealed (Isa. 56:1).

Today salvation comes to the house of my family, because we are sons of Abraham (Luke 19:9).

The salvation of God has been sent to my family, and they will hear it (Acts 28:28).

The prophets have prophesied that the grace of salvation will come to my family (1 Pet. 1:10).

In the day of salvation the Lord has helped my family (2 Cor. 6:2).

Now is the day of salvation for my family (2 Cor. 6:2).

My family smiles at their enemies because they rejoice in the salvation of the Lord (1 Sam. 2:1).

Today the Lord has accomplished salvation in my family (1 Sam. 11:13).

The Lord is the shield and horn of salvation for my family. He saves us from violence (2 Sam. 22:3).

Although my family is not so with God, He has made us an everlasting covenant. This is our salvation, and He will make it increase (2 Sam. 23:5).

The Lord will increase the salvation of my family (2 Sam. 23:5).

My family glorifies the Lord and orders their conduct aright; therefore He will show us His salvation (Ps. 50:23).

The Lord is salvation for my family in the time of trouble (Isa. 33:2).

My family will be saved with an everlasting salvation, and we will not be ashamed or disgraced (Isa. 45:17).

The Lord's salvation for my family is from generation to generation (Isa. 51:8).

The gospel of Christ is the power of salvation to my family (Rom. 1:16).

It is high time for my family to awake out of sleep, for now our salvation is nearer than when we first believed (Rom. 13:11).

May godly sorrow produce repentance in my family, leading them to salvation (2 Cor. 7:10).

My family trusts the Lord, after hearing the word of truth, the gospel of our salvation. We are sealed with the Holy Spirit of promise (Eph. 1:13).

My family will stand still and see the salvation of the Lord, which He will accomplish today (Exod. 14:13).

God of our salvation will save my family. He will gather us together and deliver us to give thanks to His holy name, to triumph in His praise (1 Chron. 16:35).

Violence, waste, and destruction shall no longer be heard of in my family. We will call our walls salvation and our gates praise (Isa. 60:18).

The Lord has clothed my family with the garments of salvation and covered us with robes of righteousness (Isa. 61:10).

Our salvation goes forth like a lamp that burns (Isa. 62:1).

Chapter 29

FASTING TO BREAK THE STRONGHOLDS IN YOUR CITY AND NATION

God blessed them and said to them, "Be fruitful and multiply, and replenish the earth and subdue it. Rule over the fish of the sea and over the birds of the air and over every living thing that moves on the earth."

—Genesis 1:28

Behemoth: Something of oppressive or monstrous size or power.[1]

WHEN IT COMES to praying and fasting for large territories such as cities and nations, you need to have some knowledge of the spirits that control those areas and how they are defeated. I am going to talk about two territorial strongholds that oppress cities and nations—behemoth and marine demons—and the ways to pull them down.

BEHEMOTH

A behemoth is any system that is large enough in size or power to oppress multitudes of people. It can be a religious, political, cultural, or economic system. Behemoths are strongholds erected by the enemy to keep the gospel out and multitudes of people in darkness. They must be broken in order to see millions of people released from darkness and come into the glorious light of the knowledge of Jesus Christ.

The Lord is raising up an army of believers who understand spiritual warfare and will challenge and pull down the behemoths of our day.

Examples of behemoths include:

- Communism: a recent system that has been shaken, and is falling. Communism was an antichrist system that controlled millions. For years the church prayed and fasted for the dismantling of this behemoth, and now we see the results of our prayers.

- Islam: controls entire nations, enslaving millions of people through its antichrist message. The gospel is kept out by this behemoth, and millions are dying lost without a saving knowledge of Jesus Christ. It is an oppressive system that enslaves multitudes to its rigid code of religious law. The good news is that the behemoth of Islam will fall just as the behemoth of Communism is falling, and the gospel will be preached to those people for whom Jesus died.

- Roman Catholic Church: In the days of Martin Luther, this religious behemoth controlled kings, governments, and entire nations of people. The word of the pope was supreme, and he was considered to be the voice of Christ on the earth. He was considered infallible, and he had the right to install, approve, or disapprove of kings and rulers. The Roman Catholic Church had absolute authority in church matters, to establish and set doctrine, to ordain and install ministers (priesthood), to excommunicate members considered heretics, etc. Those who disagreed with the teachings of the church were not only subject to excommunication but also death.

The gospel of Jesus Christ always produces liberty. Behemoths resist the gospel and the truth of Jesus Christ and attempt to keep people in bondage. Behemoth denies religious freedom, fights the existence of the church, and tries to control the church.

In categorizing strongholds, saints need to understand that some come under the category of a behemoth. This stronghold cannot be attacked like others because of the sheer size and magnitude of its strength. This size can include geographical, monetary, political, and military strength. It took years to pray and dismantle the behemoth of Communism.

Man, in his own strength, cannot tame or capture behemoths. Only God who created them can tame and subdue them. Persistence and patience are necessary in pulling down a behemoth. Prayer, fasting, and often martyrdom are necessary to destroy a behemoth.

MARINE DEMONS

Man was given dominion over the fish of the sea and over the fowl of the air. Man lost his dominion through sin. Satan came into the earth through Adam's sin. The earth and the waters were affected by the Fall.

The class of demons that operate from water are called marine demons. Marine demons are very high ranking in Satan's overall kingdom and affect land when men invite them through "conscious" or "unconscious" pacts and decisions. These spirits represent witchcraft, lust, perversion, murder, death, pride, rebellion, destruction, and greed. Coastal areas are vulnerable to these spirits, and churches in these areas need to be aware of their activities. God's power is needed today to muzzle them just as God did in the beginning. Those involved in spiritual warfare should not overlook this key component of Satan's kingdom.

Water is a symbol of life. There can be no life apart from water. It should not be surprising that demons would pervert this truth and use the waters to bring destruction. There has been violence, blood, murder, rape, slavery, and thievery within our oceans. Thousands of slaves were thrown overboard through the slave trade. Wealth, including gold and silver, has been transported across the oceans, after lands were plundered. Illegal drugs have been transported across the seas. Marine spirits promote murder and greed. Bloodshed causes defilement. Many waters have been defiled by blood, which gives marine spirits strength to operate. There have been many covenants made with spirits connected to the waters (Isa. 28:17).

Waterways are gateways to cities and nations. Satan will always try to possess the gates. He will place some of his strongest demons at these gates. Gates control the flow in and out of a region. We are to possess the gates of the enemy. We can command the gates to open for the King of glory to enter (Ps. 24:7).

Coastal cities and island nations are strongholds for marine demons.

> Woe to the inhabitants of the seacoast…
>
> —ZEPHANIAH 2:5

Many cities in America located on large bodies of water such as San Francisco, Los Angeles, New York, Miami, New

Orleans, and Chicago are strongholds of perversion, violence, drug addiction, witchcraft, and rebellion. Cities such as Amsterdam, Rio de Janeiro, Istanbul, Cape Town, and Mumbai are international examples of cities controlled by marine spirits. These cities are gateway cities that include ports. There is a great degree of spiritual traffic through these gateways. Marine spirits must be challenged and bound if we are to see revival come to these cities.

Spirits represented by sea creatures

- ✦ Mind-binding and mind-controlling spirits that have the form of a squid or an octopus. These spirits have tentacles that wrap around the minds of people, hindering them from thinking clearly. These spirits cause much confusion and keep people from seeing the truth. These are powerful spirits that often require fasting to break.

- ✦ Spirits of lust and perversion can often take the form of frogs.

- ✦ The spirit of pride takes the form of a large sea serpent, Leviathan.

- ✦ Some evil spirits are represented by flying fish and birds that swim (Gen. 1:20). Some birds live in water (stork and heron, both unclean birds—Deut. 14:18).

God is angry with these entities operating from the waters and He will judge them (Zech. 10:11). These proud entities must bow to the power of God. We can release God's judgment and anger against them.

God desires to deliver those who are controlled by these spirits. Water, which is a symbol of life, is turned into death through the operation of these spirits. People under the influence of these spirits feel as if they are drowning in many waters.

There are many scriptures that refer to deliverance from waters, floods, and depths (Ps. 18:14–17; 69:1–2; 93:3–4; 124:4–5; 130:1; 144:6–7). These scriptures can be used in casting out marine spirits.

People bound by perversion, pride, lust, and witchcraft are often controlled by marine spirits. Sever all ties with the marine kingdom and command the spirits to come out. Release the judgments written against them in Scripture and release the captives. Break any covenants with the marine kingdom made by ancestors. Break the curses of pride and witchcraft common with marine spirits. Sever all ties with leviathan, Rahab, and Babylon. Release the sword of the Lord against them and command all evil waters to dry up.

Fasting is another powerful tool against marine spirits. Marine spirits are strong and some will only be defeated through fasting.

100 POINTS ON WHICH TO PRAY AND FAST FOR YOUR CITY

Do you want to see changes in your city, region, and nation? This is your right and inheritance as a son or daughter of the King. As you pray, your Father will give you nations for an inheritance (Ps. 2:8). Your prayers have the power to change geographic regions (Eccles. 8:4).

1. Pray for Jesus to be glorified.
2. Pray for evangelistic anointing to increase in your city.
3. Pray for apostolic breakthrough believers to increase.
4. Pray for the level of worship to increase.
5. Pray for miracles and power of God to increase.
6. Pray for immorality to be restrained in churches.
7. Pray for godly leaders to lead in churches.
8. Pray for an increase in finances for churches.
9. Pray for the prophetic to increase in your region.
10. Pray for deliverance to increase in your region.
11. Pray for sound doctrine and teaching to increase.
12. Pray for the youth to be ignited for revival.
13. Pray for the government of your region.
14. Pray for witchcraft and sorcery to be destroyed.
15. Pray for church growth.
16. Pray for land and property to be released.
17. Pray for unity between churches.
18. Pray for strife and division to be destroyed.
19. Pray for carnality to be destroyed in churches.
20. Pray for anointed ministries to be released.
21. Pray for healing of sickness to increase.
22. Pray for anointed preaching of the Word.
23. Pray for revelation to be increased.

24. Pray for order in the churches.

25. Pray for pastors and their families.

26. Pray for men to come into the kingdom.

27. Pray for marriages.

28. Pray for the unmarried.

29. Pray for revival in schools and colleges.

30. Pray for perversion to be rebuked.

31. Pray for violence and death to be restrained.

32. Pray against poverty and lack.

33. Pray against gang violence and drug addiction.

34. Pray against foreclosures and property loss.

35. Pray against terrorism.

36. Pray against weather disasters.

37. Pray against mass shootings.

38. Pray against corruption and theft.

39. Pray against mental illness.

40. Pray for transportation systems.

41. Pray against excessive taxation.

42. Pray against false ministries in your region.

43. Pray against the spirit of control in churches.

44. Pray for backsliders to return to God.

45. Pray for the kingdom to advance in your region.

46. Pray for the right people to be elected.

47. Pray for the Holy Spirit to be poured out.

48. Pray for unusual miracles and visitations.

49. Pray for mass conversions.

50. Pray for the media to be opened for churches.

51. Pray for ungodly laws to be stopped and overturned.

52. Pray for the righteous to be promoted.

53. Pray for the wicked to be exposed.

54. Pray for favor for churches and ministries.

55. Pray against witches and the occult.

56. Pray for angelic intervention.

57. Pray for apostolic strategies.

58. Pray for an increase of wisdom.

59. Pray for the fear of the Lord to come into the region.

60. Pray for creative miracles.

61. Pray for economic growth in your region.

62. Pray for new technologies.

63. Pray for racial reconciliation.

64. Pray against racism and injustice.

65. Pray for the release of apostolic teams.

66. Pray against lukewarmness in churches.

67. Pray against false religions and temples.

68. Pray for widows.

69. Pray for the elderly.

70. Pray for the homeless.

71. Pray against abortion and murder.

72. Pray against teen pregnancy and illegitimacy.

73. Pray for inner cities to be rebuilt.

74. Pray for people incarcerated.

75. Pray for emerging ministries.

76. Pray for Bible schools and ministry training.

77. Pray for Christian bookstores and businesses.

78. Pray for visions and dreams to manifest.

79. Pray for love to increase.

80. Pray for ushers and helps ministries.

81. Pray for children's church.

82. Pray for police and fire departments.

83. Pray for military bases.

84. Pray for hospitals and nursing homes.

85. Pray against crime and vice.

86. Pray for family restoration.

87. Pray against unemployment.

88. Pray for safety and protection of cities.

89. Pray to expose satanic and demonic agendas.

90. Pray for anointed psalmists and minstrels.

91. Pray for church administrators.

92. Pray for the creative and godly arts.

93. Pray for new things to be released.

94. Pray for God's mercy over our cities.

95. Pray against legalism and religious bondage.

96. Pray for honor to be restored to the church.

97. Pray against church and ministry scandals.

98. Pray for the gates of the city to be opened to the King.

99. Pray for the gatekeepers of the city/region.

100. Pray for revival.

PRAYERS AGAINST TERRORISM

I bind and rebuke every red eagle of terror that would come against my nation in the name of Jesus (Jer. 49:22).

I will not be afraid of the terror by night (Ps. 91:5).

I bind and rebuke all terrorists that would plot against my nation in the name of Jesus.

I bind and rebuke all spirits of hatred and murder that would manifest through terrorism in the name of Jesus.

I bind and rebuke all religious terrorists in the name of Jesus.

I bind and rebuke all demons of jihad in the name of Jesus.

I bind and rebuke all spirits of antichrist and hatred of Christianity in the name of Jesus.

I bind all spirits of hatred of America in the name of Jesus.

I bind and rebuke the terrors of death in the name of Jesus (Ps. 55:4).

I bind all fear and panic that would come through terrorism in the name of Jesus.

Deliver me from violent and bloodthirsty men (Ps. 140:1).

I cut the acts of violence out of the hands of the wicked (Isa. 59:6).

Let the assemblies of violent men be exposed and cut off (Ps. 86:14).

Let violence be no more in my borders (Isa. 60:18).

Prayers for Your Nation

I pray for the leaders of my nation to come to the light (Isa. 60:3).

I make supplication, prayer, intercession, and give thanks for all the people of my nation and for the leaders of my nation, that I might live a peaceable life in all godliness and honesty (1 Tim. 2:1–2).

Let our leaders be just, and let them rule by the fear of the Lord (2 Sam. 23:3).

Let our leaders fall down before the Lord, and let my nation serve Him (Ps. 72:11).

Let the poor and needy people of my nation be delivered (Ps. 72:12–13).

Let the Lord's dominion be established in my nation, and let His enemies lick the dust (Ps. 72:8–9).

Turn our leaders' hearts to fear You (Prov. 21:1).

Let the Lord rule over my nation, and let my nation be glad and rejoice (Ps. 97:1).

Let my nation sing a new song, bless His name, and show forth His salvation from day to day (Ps. 96:1–3).

Let the people of my nation tremble at the presence of the Lord (Ps. 99:1).

Let my nation make a joyful noise to the Lord, and let the people serve Him with gladness (Ps. 110:1–2).

Let our leaders praise You, and let them hear the words of Your mouth (Ps. 138:4).

Let the wicked be rooted out of our land (Prov. 2:22).

Let the wicked be cut down and wither as the green herb (Ps. 37:2).

Let all the people of my nation turn to the Lord and worship Him (Ps. 22:27).

My nation is the Lord's and the fullness thereof, and all they that dwell therein (Ps. 24:1).

Let all the idolaters in my nation be confounded, and let all the gods worship the Lord (Ps. 97:7).

Let my nation praise the Lord for His merciful kindness and truth (Ps. 117).

Save my nation, O Lord, and send prosperity (Ps. 118:25).

I pray that my nation will submit to the rule and reign of Christ (Dan. 7:14).

I pray my nation will bring its wealth into the kingdom (Rev. 21:24).

I pray my nation will be converted and bring its wealth to the King (Isa. 60:5).

I pray my nation will be healed by the leaves from the tree of life (Rev. 22:2).

I pray my nation will show forth the praises of God (Isa. 60:6).

I pray my nation will see the glory of God (Isa. 35:2).

Let those who are deaf hear the words of the book, and let the blind see out of obscurity (Isa. 29:18).

I pray that Jesus will rule over my nation in righteousness and judgment (Isa. 32:1).

I pray my nation will come to Zion to be taught, and learn war no more (Isa. 2:1–4).

I pray that my nation will seek the Lord and enter into His rest (Isa. 11:1).

I pray that the parched places in my nation will become a pool, and every thirsty part springs of water (Isa. 35:7).

I pray that the glory of the Lord be revealed to my nation, and that all the inhabitants will see it (Isa. 40:5).

Let the Lord bring righteousness and judgment to my nation (Isa. 42:1).

I ask the Lord to do a new thing in my nation by giving waters in the wilderness and streams in the desert (Isa. 43:19–20).

Let peace (shalom) come into my nation like a river (Isa. 66:12).

Let my nation be sprinkled by the blood of Jesus (Isa. 52:12).

Let the children of my nation be taught of the Lord (Isa. 54:13).

I pray that my nation will seek and find the Lord (Isa. 65:1).

Let my nation be filled with priests and Levites that worship the Lord (Isa. 66:21).

Let the people of my nation come and worship the Lord (Isa. 66:23).

Let my people build houses and inhabit them (Isa. 65:21).

Let my people plant vineyards and eat the fruit of them (Isa. 65:21).

Let my people long enjoy the work of their hands (Isa. 65:22).

Let the enemies in my land be reconciled (Isa. 65:25).

Let my nation be filled with the knowledge of the glory of the Lord (Hab. 2:14).

Let my nation be saved and walk in the light of Zion (Rev. 21:24).

Let God be merciful unto us and bless us, and cause His face to shine upon us. Let His way be known to us, and His saving health in our nation (Ps. 67:1–2).

Let every covenant with death and hell be broken in our nation (Isa. 28:18).

Let my nation look to the Lord and be saved (Isa. 45:22).

Let the Lord make bare His holy arm, and let my nation see the salvation of the Lord (Isa. 52:10).

Let every veil spread over my nation be destroyed (Isa. 25:7).

My nation is the inheritance of the Lord; let Him possess it (Ps. 2:7–8).

The kingdom is the Lord's, and He is the governor of my nation (Ps. 22:28).

Let the people who walk in darkness in my nation see the light, and let Your light shine upon those in the shadow of darkness (Isa. 9:2).

Let His government and peace (shalom) continually increase in my nation (Isa. 9:7).

Let His justice and judgment increase in my nation (Isa. 9:7).

Let those in my nation who were not Your people be called the children of the living God (Rom. 9:25–26).

Let righteousness, peace, and joy in the Holy Ghost increase in my nation (Rom. 14:17).

Chapter 30

FASTING FOR THE ANOINTING ON YOUR LIFE

*But in all things we commend ourselves as
ministers of God, in much patience . . . in fastings.*

—2 CORINTHIANS 6:4–5, NKJV

ASTING IS ONE of the ways we approve ourselves as ministers of God. Every believer is a minister. All believers minister salvation, healing, and deliverance to others. Fasting is one of the ways we approve ourselves as ministers of God. God's ministers are expected to fast. A minister who will not fast is not approving himself. Fasting is one of the ways we prove ourselves genuine ministers of God.

Fasting should be part of any genuine apostolic and prophetic ministry. Apostolic and prophetic people need the grace that results from fasting to pioneer and break through. Fasting helps release revelation and insight into the plans and purposes of God.

FASTING GIVES YOU SPIRITUAL STRENGTH

The LORD is my light and my salvation; whom will I fear?
The LORD is the strength of my life; of whom will I be
afraid?

—PSALM 27:1

Food is what gives us physical strength. When you fast you are depriving yourself of what gives you physical strength. You are in essence saying, "The Lord is the strength of my life."

As a believer and minister of God, you must understand

that you cannot serve God in your own strength. Fasting helps you tap into the strength of God. You spirit will become stronger through fasting, and this will help you overcome the weakness of the flesh.

I recommend fasting when you feel tired and burnt out, especially if this is due to ministering. Fasting actually gives your digestive system a rest and will help you overcome tiredness and weariness. Ministry releases a lot of virtue, and you must be careful not to begin to depend on your strength and your flesh in doing ministry.

FASTING: MAN SHALL NOT LIVE BY BREAD ALONE

> He humbled you and let you suffer hunger, and fed you with manna, which you did not know, nor did your fathers know, that He might make you know that man does not live by bread alone; but man lives by every word that proceeds out of the mouth of the LORD.
>
> —DEUTERONOMY 8:3

God suffered Israel to hunger by feeding them with manna for forty years. He did this to make them know that man does not live by bread only, but by every word that proceeds out of the mouth of the Lord.

> Jesus answered him, "It is written, 'Man shall not live by bread alone, but by every word of God.'"
>
> —LUKE 4:4

Jesus quoted from this verse in Deuteronomy while concluding His forty-day fast, while being tempted of the devil. When you fast, you are declaring that, "I do not live by bread only, but by every word that proceeds out of the mouth of the Lord."

Fasting will help you receive and live by the Word of God. Fasting will help you understand and receive the deeper truth of the Word. Fasting will open the way for you to walk in greater revelation of the Word. This is just what you need to be an effective minister of God.

Fasting will release the Holy Spirit and increase prophetic anointing.

> And it will be that, afterwards, I will pour out My Spirit on all flesh; then your sons and your daughters will prophesy, your old men will dream dreams, and your young men will see visions.
>
> —JOEL 2:28

Fasting will help to release the power of the prophetic anointing over your life through the Holy Spirit. This is one of the greatest promises given by the prophet Joel—that God would pour out His Spirit over you, and you will prophesy, dream dreams, and see visions. The context of this verse in Joel 2 is that the people of Israel had been instructed to fast (see verse 12). It is at the end of this period of fasting that the Lord made the promise in verse 28. This is the promise of the last-day outpouring of the Holy Spirit. Fasting helps to release the manifestation of prophecy. Fasting also helps release visions and dreams. The word of the Lord is health and life to your spirit. Fasting will release the power of the Holy Spirit for the miraculous to occur.

> Jesus returned in the power of the Spirit to Galilee. And His fame went throughout the surrounding region.... "The

> Spirit of the Lord is upon Me, because He has anointed Me to preach the gospel to the poor; He has sent Me to heal the broken-hearted, to preach deliverance to the captives and recovery of sight to the blind, to set at liberty those who are oppressed."
>
> —LUKE 4:14, 18

Fasting increases the anointing and the power of the Holy Spirit in the life of a believer. Jesus ministered in power after fasting. He healed the sick and cast out devils. All believers are expected to do the same works (John 14:12). Fasting helps us to minister healing and deliverance to our families and others around us. Fasting helps us walk in the power of God. Fasting releases the anointing for miracles to happen.

DECLARATIONS TO RELEASE THE GIFT OF HEALING

I pray that God would anoint me to have virtue in my life—not only in my hands but also in my clothes so that wherever I go and encounter sick people, they will be healed when I touch them.

Heavenly Father, I receive an anointing for healing in my hands and in my body. Let virtue be released through me and through my clothing. Let Your power be released through me so that wherever I go people will be healed.

Heavenly Father, as I fast and pray, increase Your healing virtue in my body and in my clothing, that wherever I go and whoever I touch will be healed.

I believe for miracles to flow through my life in Jesus's name.

SUBMITTING YOURSELF TO GOD'S SERVICE

The people are crying for You, Lord. Anoint me like You anointed Benjamin. Send me to this land as a spiritual captain over Your people, that they might be saved out of the hand of the enemy (1 Sam. 9:16).

You have anointed me and delivered me from the hands of my enemies, just as You did for King David (2 Sam. 12:7).

I will arise and be cleansed. I will be clothed by the Holy Spirit. I will be anointed as I worship in Your house. I will eat of the bread of life from the table that You have set before me (2 Sam. 12:20).

Turn Your face toward me, O God, and remember Your mercy toward me as one You have anointed (2 Chron. 6:42).

In Your love for righteousness and hatred of wickedness, You have anointed me with the oil of gladness more than all those around me (Ps. 45:7; Heb. 1:9).

You have anointed me with fresh oil, and now I am strong as a wild ox (Ps. 92:10).

Turn Your face toward me, Your anointed (Ps. 132:10).

My burden shall be taken away from off my shoulder, and the yoke removed from off my neck and destroyed, because of the anointing upon my life (Isa. 10:27).

PRAYERS FOR PERSONAL ANOINTING

Just as the Lord gave a specific anointing to Aaron, by reason of the anointing, I have also been given a specific ministry gift to use, which shall be mine—and my children's—by God's ordinance forever (Num. 18:8).

I know that the Lord saves His anointed, and He will hear me when I call and will come to my aid with the saving strength of His right hand (Ps. 20:6).

God has prepared a table before me in the presence of mine enemies: He has anointed my head with oil; my cup runs over (Ps. 23:5).

The Lord is my strength, and, as His anointed, I will be saved by His strength (Ps. 28:8).

Just like the blind man whom Jesus told to wash in the pool of Siloam, I will demand that God's anointing power will flow through His servants today and touch my eyes, so that I may wash and receive spiritual sight (John 9:11).

Lord, keep Your eyes upon Your faithful servants in this land, that we may dwell with You, and help us to walk in a perfect way so that we may serve You and cause many to seek Your anointing also (Ps. 101:6).

Father, make me like Stephen—full of faith and power—that I may do great wonders and miracles among the people (Acts 6:8).

I will stay full of the Holy Ghost and of faith so that many will say, "He was a good man," and because of Your anointing on my life many people will be added unto the Lord (Acts 11:24).

I have been anointed to open their eyes and to turn them from darkness to light, and from the power of Satan unto God, that they may receive forgiveness of sins and inheritance among those who are sanctified by faith that is in me (Acts 26:18).

I thank Christ Jesus our Lord, who has enabled me, for counting me faithful and putting me into the ministry (1 Tim. 1:12).

I work miracles according to the hearing of faith and not by the works of the law (Gal. 3:5).

God has called me, and He is faithful to do through me that for which I was called (1 Thess. 5:24).

I will receive strength to conceive that seed of the dreams, anointing, and gifts that God has placed in me. I declare in faith that those same dreams, anointing, and gifts will be delivered, because God, who has promised, has declared me faithful (Heb. 11:11).

The anointing of God abides in me and teaches me all things. The anointing reveals the truth to me as I abide in God (1 John 2:27).

I offer excellent sacrifices before You, O God, because You have counted me righteous by my faith. Testify of the gifts You have anointed me with, that even after I am dead my eternal works will speak (Heb. 11:4).

I will obey God and, by faith, go to where He has called me so I may receive my inheritance (Heb. 11:8).

PROPHET WITHOUT HONOR: PRAYERS AGAINST HOMETOWN SPIRITS

And they took offense at Him. But Jesus said to them, "A prophet is not without honor except in his own country and in his own house." And He did not do many mighty works there because of their unbelief.

—MATTHEW 13:57–58

Every spirit of dishonor operating against me in my hometown, I bind and rebuke you in the name of Jesus.

Every spirit of jealousy, envy operating against me in my hometown, I bind and rebuke you in the name of Jesus.

All spirits of familiarity that view me through the eyes of the natural instead of the Spirit, I bind and rebuke in the name of Jesus.

All spirits of unbelief in my gifts, calling, and anointing, be rebuked in the name of Jesus.

All spirits trying to hold my past against me in my hometown, be rebuked in the name of Jesus.

I rebuke demons in my hometown that are familiar with me and oppose and fight against me.

Chapter 31

MAINTAINING BREAKTHROUGH AND DELIVERANCE

Therefore if the Son sets you free, you shall be free indeed.

—JOHN 8:36

SEASONS OF FASTING and prayer are important parts of a believer's life, especially for those who are involved in deliverance ministry and who are seeking deliverance for themselves. Fasting leads to victory and deliverance from strongholds and brings greater levels of spiritual strength and maturity. Deliverance is from God and is part of the blessing of being in covenant with Him. It only destroys what is of the devil; it never destroys what is of the Holy Spirit. Since deliverance is a work of the Holy Spirit, it builds up the saints and edifies the church. It tears down the strongholds of the enemy, but builds up the work of God. Deliverance will strengthen you and prepare you for a greater manifestation of God's power. Fasting brings breakthrough and deliverance. The next process after fasting is to continue to live your life from the place of freedom that you have just acquired.

One of the main keys to maintaining deliverance that is obtained after a season of fasting and prayer is by activating the spiritual gift of self-control. Fasting and prayer give you the discernment and strength you need to be vigilant in identifying and eradicating the areas of your life that were out of control. Do not go back to a lifestyle where you are easily carried away, disorderly, out of hand, rebellious, uncontrollable, ungovernable, unmanageable, unruly, or undisciplined. The Holy Spirit is your compass and magnifying glass in this area. An undisciplined lifestyle will bring you right back into bondage. There is no lasting deliverance and freedom without discipline.

> He who has no rule over his own spirit is like a city that is broken down and without walls.
>   —Proverbs 25:28

The Common English Bible translates Proverbs 25:28 like this: "A person without self-control is like a breached city, one with no walls." Cities without walls were open to invasion and attack from outside forces. A person without self-control is open for demons.

To maintain your deliverance, you need to have self-control in these areas:

1. Thinking. Philippians 4:8 says, "Finally, brothers, whatever things are true, whatever things are honest, whatever things are just, whatever things are pure, whatever things are lovely, whatever things are of good report, if there is any virtue, and if there is any praise, think on these things."

2. Appetites. Proverbs 23:2 says, "and put a knife to your throat, if you are a man given to appetite."

3. Speaking. Proverbs 25:28 (wyc) says, "As a city open, and without compass of walls; so is a man that may not refrain his spirit in speaking. (Like a city that is open, and without any walls surrounding it, is a man who cannot refrain his own spirit from speaking.)"

4. Sexual character. First Corinthians 9:27 says, "But I bring and keep my body under subjection, lest when preaching to others I myself should be disqualified."

5. Emotions. Proverbs 15:13 says, "A merry heart makes a cheerful countenance, but by sorrow of the heart the spirit is broken."

6. Temper. Ecclesiastes 7:9 (NKJV) says, "Do not hasten in your spirit to be angry, for anger rests in the bosom of fools."

Here's how you gain and maintain self-control, thereby maintain your freedom from bondage:

1. Read God's Word daily.

2. Find a group of Bible-believing people, preferably a church, and regularly meet with them for worship, study, and ministry.

3. Pray with the understanding and in tongues.

4. Place the blood of Jesus on yourself and your family.

5. Determine as nearly as you can which spirits have been cast out of you. Make a list for these areas Satan will try to recapture.

6. The way demons gain reentry is through a lax, undisciplined thought life. The mind is the battlefield. You must cast down imaginations, and bring every thought into the obedience of Christ (2 Cor. 10:5).

7. Pray to the Father fervently, asking Him to make you alert, sober, and vigilant against wrong thoughts (1 Pet. 5:8–9).

8. The demons signal their approach to you by the fact that the old thought patterns you once had are now

trying to return to you. As soon as this happens, immediately rebuke them. As quickly as possible state verbally that you refuse them.

9. You have the authority to loose the angels of the Lord to battle the demons (Heb. 1:14; Matt. 18:18). Bind the demons and loose upon them the spirits of destruction (1 Chron. 21:12), burning and judgment (Isa. 4:4), from the Lord Jesus Christ. Loose warrior angels upon the demons.

HOUSE CLEANING

There are times when your home has been the seat of evil or perverse activity. Sometimes dark forces may have come into your home through practices or behaviors you allowed or those that may have been forced on you. Other times they could be lingering spirits from previous residents. It's good to do some spiritual housecleaning as the Spirit of God leads you.

You may feel a strong sense of discernment and alertness in the spirit after going through personal deliverance at church or in your small group or during times of fasting and prayer. Get some anointing oil and go through your home and begin to pray scriptures and/or prayers like the ones in this book that apply to the spirits the Holy Spirit has alerted you to. If you are a new believer, I recommend that you ask a more mature believer or a deliverance minister from your church to come to your home and accompany you as you go through your home expelling and uprooting these spirits. I believe that there is strength in numbers. It may be wise, whether you are a new believer or not, to have other believers join you, especially if there have been serious problems in the home.

This is what deliverance minister Win Worley had to say about this:

> Some houses and apartments need to be cleaned of evil spirits. You would do well to check secondhand cars, homes, and apartments because if the former owners had Ouija boards, or other occultic paraphernalia, or were involved in serious bondage to sin, then there is every reason to suspect that evil spirits could be lingering behind.
>
> Believers can enter the premises reading verses of Scripture aloud in unison. Pray for discernment and for God to reveal objects that need to be removed and destroyed. Look for such things as idols, incense, Buddha or other statues, hand carved objects from Africa, the Orient or other foreign countries, Ouija boards, anything connected with astrology or horoscopes, fortune telling materials, books or objects associated with witchcraft, good luck charms, books on cult religions, rock and roll records and tapes, etc. In some cases, the door lintel and window sills should be anointed with oil. Do not overlook the dark places where spirits like to hide such as closets, attics, basements, crawl spaces, cupboards, etc.[1]

MEDITATING ON THE WORD KEEPS YOU FROM FALLING BACK INTO OPPRESSION

When you are set free through deliverance, your spirit is made alive to the things of God. Meditation keeps you from falling back into a place of darkness and oppression that cuts you off from God. Meditation maintains your position of abiding in the vine—the place of fruitfulness and life. Meditation on the Word of God is also an act of constantly keeping before you the image and character of God. This brings life to your mortal body (Rom. 8:11) and keeps you in a constant state of getting stronger and becoming more alive in Christ. By contemplating the glory of God, we go from glory to glory and faith to faith (2 Cor. 3:18). By beholding, by meditating on God's Word, we become changed and immune to the traps of the enemy.

MEDITATION DECLARATIONS

I will meditate also of all the Lord's work and talk of His doings (Ps. 77:12).

I will meditate on the Lord's precepts and contemplate His ways (Ps. 119:15).

Princes also did sit and speak against me, but I meditate on the Lord's statutes (Ps. 119:23).

Let the proud be ashamed; for they dealt perversely with me without a cause: but I will meditate in thy precepts (Ps. 119:78).

My eyes are awake during the night watches, so that I may meditate on the Lord's Word (Ps. 119:148).

I remember the days of old; I meditate on all thy works; I muse on the work of thy hands (Ps. 143:5).

I meditate upon these things; give myself wholly to them; that my profiting may appear to all (1 Tim. 4:15).

I love the law of the Lord; it is my meditation all the day (Ps. 119:97).

The law of the Lord is my delight, and in His law I meditate day and night (Ps. 1:2).

I shall be made to understand the way of the Lord's precepts, so I shall meditate on His wonderful works (Ps. 119:27).

I will remember the days of old and meditate on all the Lord's works. I will muse on the work of Your hands (Ps. 143:5).

I will lift my hands up to the Lord's commandments, which I love, and will meditate on His statutes (Ps. 119:48).

A book of remembrance will be written for me, who fears the Lord and meditates on His name (Mal. 3:16).

I will meditate on the book of the law day and night (Josh. 1:8).

NOTES

Chapter 9—Fasting to Break the Spirits of Procrastination, Passivity, and Slothfulness

1. Jean Calvin, *Institutes of the Christian Religion Volume 1* (n.p.: Hardpress, 2013), 296.

Chapter 11—Fasting for Deliverance From Bitterness, Anger, and Unforgiveness

1. Strong's Concordance, s.v. "*marah*," accessed September 10, 2015, http://biblehub.com/hebrew/4784.htm.

Chapter 12—Fasting for Victory Over Anxiety and Depression

1. Anthony L. Komaroff, "The Gut-Brain Connection", *Harvard Health Letter*, accessed September 1, 2015, http://www.health .harvard.edu/healthbeat/the-gut-brain-connection.

2. Adam Hadhazy, "Think Twice: How the Gut's 'Second Brain' Influences Mood and Well-Being," ScientificAmerican.com, February 12, 2010, accessed September 1, 2015, http://www.scientificamerican .com/article/gut-second-brain/.

Chapter 14—Fasting to Break Free From a Painful Past

1. Merriam Webster Online, s.v. "trauma," accessed September 1, 2015, http://www.merriam-webster.com/dictionary/trauma.

Chapter 16—Fasting for Victory Over Gluttony and Overindulgence

1. Brett and Kate McKay, "The Virtuous Life: Moderation," ArtofManliness.com, April 27, 2008, accessed September 1, 2015, http://www.artofmanliness.com/2008/04/27/the-virtuous-life -moderation/.

Chapter 20—Fasting to Break the Power of Witchcraft, Mind Control, and Ungodly Soul Ties

1. Derek Prince, The Seeking of Control, accessed September 10, 2015, www.scribd.com/doc/32202545/The-Seeking-of-Control-Rev-Derek-Prince.

Chapter 22—Fasting to Break the Spirit of Carnality and Double-Mindedness

1. Bruce E. Levine, "How Teenage Rebellion Has Become a Mental Illness," AlterNet, accessed September, 10, 2015, http://www.alternet.org/story/75081/how_teenage_rebellion_has_become_a_mental_illness.

Chapter 24—Fasting to Break Chronic Cycles of Backsliding

1. Strong's Concordance, s.v. "meshubah," accessed September 3, 2015, http://biblehub.com/hebrew/4878.htm

2. Strong's Concordance, s.v. "sarar," accessed September 3, 2015, http://biblehub.com/hebrew/5637.htm.

3. Strong's Concordance, s.v. "shobab," accessed September 3, 2015, http://biblehub.com/hebrew/7726.htm; s.v. "shobeb," accessed September 3, 2015, http://biblehub.com/hebrew/7728.htm.

Chapter 29—Fasting to Break the Strongholds in Your City and Nation

1. Merriam Webster Online, s.v. "behemoth," accessed September 8, 2015, http://www.merriam-webster.com/dictionary/behemoth.

Chapter 31—Maintaining Breakthrough and Deliverance

1. Win Worley, Battling the Hosts of Hell, (N.p.: H.B.C. Publications, 1976).

CONNECT WITH US!

CHARISMA HOUSE

(Spiritual Growth)

Facebook.com/CharismaHouse

@CharismaHouse

Instagram.com/CharismaHouse

(Health)

Pinterest.com/CharismaHouse

REALMS

(Fiction)

Facebook.com/RealmsFiction